Managing Editor, Sports Illustrated Kids **Mark Bechtel**

Creative Director **Beth Bugler**

Project Editor **Andrea Woo**

Director of Photography **Marguerite Schropp Lucarelli**

Photo Editor **Annmarie Avila**

Writers **Gary Gramling, Peter Martin, Jeremy Repanich, Christina M. Tapper**

Editors **Justin Tejada, Julia Morrill**

Copy Editor **Megan Collins**

Designer **Kirsten Sorton**

Imaging **Geoffrey Michaud, Dan Larkin, Robert Thompson**

TIME INC. BOOKS
Publisher: Margot Schupf
Associate Publisher: Allison Devlin
Vice President, Finance: Terri Lombardi
Executive Director, Marketing Services: Carol Pittard
Executive Director, Business Development: Suzanne Albert
Executive Publishing Director: Megan Pearlman
Associate Director of Publicity: Courtney Greenhalgh
Assistant General Counsel: Andrew Goldberg
Assistant Director, Special Sales: Ilene Schreider
Assistant Director, Production: Susan Chodakiewicz
Senior Manager, Sales Marketing: Danielle Costa
Senior Manager, Children's Category Marketing: Amanda Lipnick
Associate Prepress Manager: Alex Voznesenskiy
Assistant Project Manager: Hillary Leary

Editorial Director: Stephen Koepp
Executive Editor, Children's Books: Beth Sutinis
Art Director: Gary Stewart
Art Director, Children's Books: Georgia Morrissey
Senior Editor: Alyssa Smith
Assistant Art Director: Anne-Michelle Gallero
Copy Chief: Rina Bander
Assistant Managing Editor: Gina Scauzillo
Editorial Assistant: Courtney Mifsud

Special thanks: Allyson Angle, Brad Beatson, Jeremy Biloon, Ian Chin, Rose Cirrincione, Pat Datta, Alison Foster, Joan L. Garrison, Erika Hawxhurst, Kristina Jutzi, David Kahn, Jean Kennedy, Seniqua Koger, Amy Mangus, Melissa Presti, Kate Roncinske, Babette Ross, Dave Rozzelle, Larry Wicker

ISBN 10: 1-61893-079-6
ISBN 13: 978-1-61893-079-8
Library of Congress Control Number: 2013935640

Sports Illustrated Kids is a trademark of Time Inc.
We welcome your comments and suggestions about Sports Illustrated Kids Books.
Please write to us at:
    Sports Illustrated Kids Books
    Attention: Book Editors
    P.O. Box 361095
    Des Moines, IA 50336-1095

If you would like to order any of our hardcover Collector's Edition books, please call us at 800-327-6388 (Monday through Friday, 7 a.m. to 9 p.m., Central Time).

Fenway Park, home of the Boston Red Sox, is our Number 1 spot to watch a game.

The Top 10 Lists

Gymnast Gabrielle Douglas, one of our Top 10 underdog stories, wowed crowds as she won the Olympic all-around gold medal at the 2012 Games in London.

Top 10
Championship

Games *since 2000*

1

Super Bowl XLII (2008)
New York Giants vs. New England Patriots

The New York Giants entered the Super Bowl as heavy underdogs, facing a New England Patriots team that was undefeated in the 2007 season. But the Giants rose to the occasion, using a pass rush powered by defensive end Justin Tuck to sack Patriots quarterback Tom Brady five times. The fourth quarter saw three lead changes, with the Giants taking control as the clock wound down. With about a minute left and New York down 14–10, Giants QB Eli Manning completed a pass to receiver David Tyree, who trapped the ball against his helmet for a first down. Four plays later, Manning connected with Plaxico Burress in the end zone to pull off the upset and win the Super Bowl 17–14.

2

2004 American League Championship Series
Boston Red Sox vs. New York Yankees

It looked as if the Curse of the Bambino — the jinx that had kept the Red Sox from winning the World Series ever since they sold Babe Ruth to the New York Yankees after the 1919 season — was about to strike again. At the 2004 ALCS, Boston was three outs from getting swept by its archrival, and then the unimaginable happened. Facing closer Mariano Rivera, Boston tied the game and won in extra innings behind a walk-off home run by David Ortiz. Boston wasn't done yet. They won the next three games, capped off by a 10–3 victory in Game 7, prompting Red Sox owner John Henry to declare the rally "the greatest comeback in baseball history." Boston rode the momentum of the historic comeback into the World Series, where the curse was finally lifted.

3 2010 NBA Finals
Los Angeles Lakers vs. Boston Celtics
The Los Angeles Lakers and the Boston Celtics wrote another chapter in their storied rivalry during the 2010 NBA Finals. The teams traded wins over the first four contests before the Celtics took the series lead in Game 5. The Celtics had never blown a 3–2 lead in the NBA Finals, but Lakers star Kobe Bryant was determined to change that. Los Angeles won the next game to force a Game 7. During the decisive game in front of a home crowd at Staples Center, Bryant helped his team rally from a 13-point deficit to beat the Celtics 83–79, making the Lakers back-to-back NBA champions.

4 2008 Wimbledon men's final
Rafael Nadal vs. Roger Federer
Roger Federer was on a quest to win his sixth consecutive Wimbledon title and his 66th straight win on grass. Rafael Nadal was looking for his first Grand Slam win not at the French Open. The rivals played an epic five-set match that lasted four hours and 48 minutes, the longest Wimbledon men's final in history. Nadal got off to a commanding two-set lead. Unrattled, Federer won the next two sets in tiebreakers, fighting off two match points, to force a fifth set. Facing cold temperatures, rain delays, and, eventually, darkness, Nadal was not about to let the match slip away. After trading service holds until 7–7 in the fifth, Nadal finally broke Federer. At 9:15 p.m., the Spaniard prevailed 6–4, 6–4, 6–7 (5), 6–7 (8), 9–7 in what some consider the greatest tennis match ever.

5 Men's ice hockey gold medal game at the 2010 Olympics
Canada vs. United States

It was one of the most dramatic games in Olympic hockey history. Team Canada, playing on home ice at the Vancouver Games, faced its North American rival, which it had lost to in the previous round. Canada jumped in front 2–0, but the U.S. would cut the lead to one in the second period. Then, with less than a minute left in the game, the U.S. pulled goalie Ryan Miller. With an extra man on the ice, forward Zach Parise tied the game to send it into overtime. That's when Canada center Sidney Crosby (87) solidified his status as hockey's golden boy and Canada's national hero. In the eighth minute of OT, he scored the golden goal with a shot from the left circle. The win gave hockey-crazed Canada its eighth Olympic gold in the sport.

8 2011 Women's World Cup final
Japan vs. United States

Japan upset host country Germany in the quarters and Sweden in the semis for a date in the final against the two-time World Cup–champion U.S. team. It proved to be a tightly contested match, with Japan coming from behind twice to tie the game. Knotted at 2–2 after overtime, the game was going to be settled by a shootout. With the pressure on, the U.S. missed three of its first four penalty kicks. In the fourth round, Saki Kumagai's kick beat U.S. goalkeeper Hope Solo to give the victory to Japan.

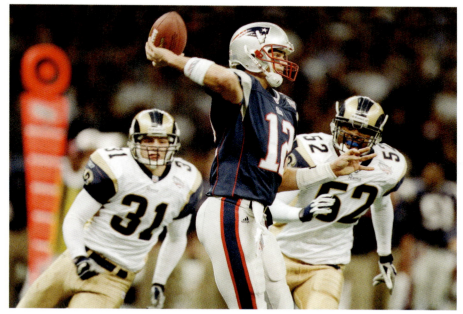

7 Super Bowl XXXVI (2002)
New England Patriots vs. St. Louis Rams

Led by unsung quarterback Tom Brady, a sixth-round pick in the 2000 draft, the 2001 Patriots made it to Super Bowl XXXVI and faced the St. Louis Rams, the team with the NFL's best record (14–2). With the game tied at 17 and 1:30 left, Brady completed a successful drive to set up kicker Adam Vinatieri for a field goal. Vinatieri nailed a 48-yarder to give the Patriots their first Super Bowl title in franchise history.

6 2008 NCAA men's basketball final
Kansas vs. Memphis

It was a battle of two Number 1 seeds in the 2008 NCAA championship game. Down by nine with 2:12 left in the game, Kansas started to mount a comeback, capitalizing on a series of missed free throws by Memphis. The Tigers clung to a three-point lead with 10.8 seconds left. Kansas then got the ball into the hands of guard Mario Chalmers, who came up big in the clutch, nailing a game-tying 3-pointer with 2.1 seconds on the clock. The shot pushed the game into overtime, where the Jayhawks took over to win 75–68 for their first NCAA title in 20 years.

9 2009 Stanley Cup finals
Pittsburgh Penguins vs. Detroit Red Wings

It was déjà vu for the Penguins and Red Wings, who had faced each other in the previous season's finals. The Pens were not about to let Detroit beat them in the Cup finals again. Facing elimination, Pittsburgh won Game 6 and played Game 7 largely without its captain, Sidney Crosby, who was hurt in the second period. With center Maxime Talbot's two goals and a last-second diving save from goalie Marc-Andre Fleury, the Penguins held on to win 2–1. Crosby, at age 21, became the youngest captain to hoist a Cup.

10 2001 World Series
Arizona Diamondbacks vs. New York Yankees

A few weeks removed from the September 11 tragedy, it was an emotional World Series for the New York Yankees. After winning back-to-back extra-inning games, the Yankees were within one win of clinching the Series. However, the Diamondbacks forced a Game 7. In the decisive game, the Yankees clung to a 2–1 lead going into the ninth inning. Arizona got the best of closer Mariano Rivera, culminating in Luis Gonzalez's bloop single with the bases loaded that won the Series for the D-backs.

TOP 10 STADIUMS

1 Fenway Park

The home of the Boston Red Sox, Fenway Park celebrated its 100th birthday in 2012, making it the oldest stadium in Major League Baseball. The park is best known for its intimate atmosphere and unconventional design. Among the unique features are the enormous leftfield wall, known as the Green Monster, and a short rightfield that ends at Pesky's Pole. The foul pole is named after Boston shortstop Johnny Pesky, whose six career home runs at Fenway were often pulled toward that pole.

2 Lambeau Field

Named after Curly Lambeau, the founder of the Green Bay Packers as well as a player and coach on the team, the field opened in 1957. Lambeau earned its reputation as a frozen tundra on December 31, 1967. With a temperature of –13 degrees, the Packers defeated the Dallas Cowboys 21–17. Officials had to shout at the end of plays because their metal whistles would have frozen to their lips. Despite the occasional subzero temperatures, raucous fans fill the stadium and help players celebrate touchdowns with the signature Lambeau Leap.

3 Madison Square Garden

The center of the New York City sports world, the Garden has hosted all kinds of sporting events, from figure skating to boxing, since it first opened in 1968. It is one of only five arenas to host the Stanley Cup finals and NBA finals in the same postseason. The self-proclaimed "world's most famous arena" is home to the Rangers, the Knicks, the St. John's men's basketball team, and the Liberty.

4 Wrigley Field

Wrigley, known as the Friendly Confines, is baseball's second-oldest ballpark. The Chicago Cubs began playing home games there in 1916, two years after it was built. The field is best known for its brick outfield walls covered in thick ivy. Wrigley did not install lights until 1988, and to this day hosts mostly day games.

5 The Rose Bowl

Located in Pasadena, California, the stadium has hosted the New Year's Day Rose Bowl game since 1923. With the San Gabriel Mountains as its dramatic backdrop, it remains the home of the marquee Bowl Championship Series game.

6 Joe Louis Arena

Even though it's named after the famed boxer and Detroit native, Joe Louis Arena is the heart of Hockeytown. The Detroit Red Wings have won four Stanley Cups since moving into the Joe in 1979.

7 Old Trafford

The largest soccer stadium in the Barclays Premier League is home to 20-time league champion Manchester United. It has proven to be a resilient stadium, sustaining two bombing raids during World War II.

8 Cowboys Stadium

An engineering marvel, the Cowboys' home is the world's largest domed stadium. Fans and players alike never miss a highlight thanks to a pair of 11,520-square-foot video screens that hang over the field.

9 Centre Court at Wimbledon

The lush grass court at the All England Lawn Tennis and Croquet Club is Wimbledon's showpiece. It doesn't host just tennis royalty but *real* royalty, with a box reserved for England's royal family.

10 Los Angeles Memorial Coliseum

The Coliseum is the only venue to have hosted the opening ceremony of the Olympics twice (1932 and '84). Now the home of the USC football team, the stadium has an Olympic cauldron that is lit during the fourth quarter of Trojans games, as well as during other important occasions.

Top 10 Signature Looks

1

Florence Griffith Joyner
Olympic sprinter, Career: 1980–88
It was hard to catch the world's fastest woman, but it wasn't hard to miss her. When Griffith Joyner broke the 100-meter world record at the 1988 U.S. Olympic Trials, she wore a purple asymmetric unitard that covered one leg and left the other one bare. The following summer, when she won three gold medals at the Seoul Olympic Games, Flo-Jo painted each of her long fingernails with a different color and design. To this day, no female track star has matched her speed or style.

2

Troy Polamalu
NFL safety, Career: 2003–present
When Polamalu played safety for USC, his locks were fluffy and distinctive but pretty much unseen when he strapped on his helmet. But after entering the NFL, the Pittsburgh Steelers star really let his hair down. And down. And down. The unruly mane grew until it flowed behind him as he swarmed the field, making him easy to spot on any play. He later insured his long locks for $1 million and became a shampoo spokesman.

3 David Beckham
Soccer midfielder,
Career: 1992–present

Before the 2002 World Cup, soccer fans knew Beckham as the runner-up for World Player of the Year in 1999 and 2001. At that Cup, he started a trend: a bleach-blond faux-hawk. The hairstyle spurred copycats from London to Tokyo, and ever since Becks has been known for being as much a fashion icon as a footballer.

4 Dennis Rodman
NBA forward,
Career: 1986–2000

Once the wild child of the NBA, Rodman combined gritty play with a flair for self-decoration. Rodman rebounded and defended his way to five NBA championships, but he became famous for dying his hair a multitude of colors, adorning himself with tattoos, and covering his head in piercings.

5 Julius Erving
ABA and NBA forward–guard,
Career: 1971–87

No single player defined the 1970s-era cool of the ABA — the rival league to the NBA before the two merged in 1976 — more than Dr. J. Before joining the NBA, Erving was the MVP in each of the ABA's last three years of existence, and his fluffy Afro and silky, gravity-defying playing style made him a basketball icon.

6 Andre Agassi
Tennis player,
Career: 1986–2006

Before he became a tennis statesman, Agassi was the sport's rebel who declared, "Image is everything." He had long hair, favored neon colors, and played matches in jean shorts. After retiring, Agassi shockingly revealed that his famous blond mullet wasn't his at all — he wore a wig to cover up the fact that he was balding!

7 Michael Jordan
NBA guard, Career: 1984–93,
'95–98, 2001–03

When Air Jordan soared for a dunk or drove past a defender, a funny thing would happen: His tongue stuck out. Soon kids were copying the look. But it was Jordan who mimicked the act in the first place. His father said in an interview that when he concentrated on home improvement projects, his tongue would jut out.

8 Brian Wilson
MLB pitcher,
Career: 2006–present

This San Francisco Giants pitcher's beard deserved to be feared. The team's closer began growing it out during the 2010 season, when he saved 48 games to help lead the Giants to a World Series crown. In the process the thick, dyed-black Brillo Pad attracted almost as much attention as Wilson's pitching.

9 Deion Sanders,
MLB outfielder/NFL cornerback,
Career: 1989–2005

Sanders didn't just play football and baseball, he put on a show. The high-stepping, trash-talking cornerback wore a headband around his neck, socks that looked like leg warmers and, of course, his do-rag. He was so fond of that accessory that when the Hall of Fame enshrined Sanders, he made sure to tie a do-rag around his bust's head.

10 Anthony Davis
NBA forward–center,
Career: 2012–present

He was the Number 1 pick in the 2012 NBA Draft, the leader of the 2011–12 NCAA champion Kentucky Wildcats, and the youngest player on Team USA at the London Olympics. But Davis became even better known for his unibrow. Some may have chosen to pluck their eyebrows, but the 6' 10" defensive star embraced his look.

Top 10

1 **Usain Bolt**
Olympic sprinter,
Career: 2004–present

When Bolt set the 100-meter world record (9.58 seconds) at the 2009 world championships, he topped out at 27.79 miles per hour to retain his title of world's fastest man. And Bolt didn't stop there. He also owns the world record in the 200 meters and was the first man to win gold medals in both events at back-to-back Olympics (2008, '12).

2 **Rickey Henderson**
MLB outfielder,
Career: 1979–2003

Henderson was an All-America running back at Oakland Technical High, but his speed's best showcase was on the base paths. No ballplayer has stolen more bases (1,406) or scored more runs (2,295) than the 5'10" outfielder. When he won the American League MVP award in 1990, he led the league in both categories.

3 **Chris Johnson**
NFL running back,
Career: 2008–present

Many athletes wonder aloud if they could challenge Usain Bolt in a race, but only Chris Johnson's boast feels legitimate. The Tennessee Titans rusher ran a lightning-quick 4.24 second 40-yard dash at the NFL scouting combine in 2008. Then he proved he wasn't just a workout wonder when he rushed for a league-leading 2,006 yards in '09.

4 **Pavel Bure**
NHL forward,
Career: 1991–2003

Opposing defenses could do little to stop Bure, who earned the nickname the Russian Rocket. In 12 seasons he led the NHL in scoring three times. Knee injuries cut Bure's career short, but he finished with the fifth highest goals-per-game average in league history and was inducted into the Hockey Hall of Fame in 2012.

5 **Michael Johnson**
Olympic sprinter,
Career: 1989–2000

When Johnson crossed the finish line of the 200-meter race at the 1996 Olympic Games, he set a record most thought would never be broken. Even though Usain Bolt bested the mark, Johnson is still the only man to win gold medals in the 200 and the 400 at the same Olympics. He did it in style, too, racing in custom gold track spikes.

Fastest

6 Secretariat
Thoroughbred,
Career: 1972–73

Only 11 horses have won the Triple Crown, and none did it in a more dominant fashion than Secretariat, who finished first in the Kentucky Derby, Preakness Stakes, and Belmont Stakes in 1973. The horse's times are still the fastest ever run in each race, including his 31-length victory (about 250 feet) in the Belmont.

7 Mario Balotelli
Soccer forward,
Career: 2006–present

Balotelli is crazy like a fox. He's as fast as one too. The AC Milan and Italian national team striker became famous for his antics, such as revealing T-shirts with strange sayings under his jersey when he scores or commissioning a statue of himself for his home. But what truly makes him unique is how he uses his speed to get behind defenses and score goals.

8 Trindon Holliday
NFL wide receiver,
Career: 2010–present

The Denver Broncos' kick-return specialist was also a star sprinter in college. When Holliday ran the 100 meters at the 2007 U.S. nationals, Peter Weyand, an expert in the science of sprinting, measured how fast Holliday moved his legs. He found that Holliday turned his legs more than six percent faster than anyone else he had ever measured.

9 Michael Phelps
Olympic swimmer,
Career: 2000–12

No swimmer has ever ruled the pool like Phelps. His 18 gold medals are twice as many as any other swimmer, and his 22 overall medals are the most by any Olympic athlete. His speed was on full display at the 2008 Summer Olympics, when he won a record-breaking eight gold medals, setting seven world records along the way.

10 Lindsey Vonn
Skier,
Career: 2000–present

America's golden girl on the slopes owns four World Cup overall titles. She races all five Alpine skiing disciplines and won Olympic gold in the downhill in 2010. Before her 2013 knee injury, Vonn petitioned to race against men. She helped her case in 2012 at a race in Canada, when her top speed (83.88 miles per hour) was faster than all but one man.

1 Cal vs. Stanford: The Play
November 20, 1982

Down 19–17 to rival California, legendary Stanford quarterback John Elway led a miracle two-minute drive to set up a field goal. The ball split the uprights with four seconds left, giving the Cardinal the lead and making the final kickoff merely a formality. Stanford celebrated so much that it was flagged for excessive celebration, pushing the kickoff back 15 yards, which didn't seem to be such a big deal. Cal's Kevin Moen took the squib kick at the 45. He scrambled and then lateraled the ball to Richard Rodgers. Rodgers quickly passed it backward to Dwight Garner. Garner was swallowed up by Stanford tacklers, and the game was over. At least that's what the Stanford bench thought. They came onto the field to celebrate — and so did all 144 members of the Stanford band. But, just before his knee hit the ground, Garner lateraled back to Rodgers. With Stanford assuming the game was over, the Bears suddenly had the advantage. Rodgers took the ball to midfield and pitched it to Mariet Ford. Ford sprinted upfield and was tripped up, but tossed the ball over his shoulder before going down. Moen caught it and dashed toward the end zone, running through the Stanford band and into the end zone, famously leaping into trombone player Gary Tyrrell after going in for the score. Officials met and determined that all the laterals were legal (many Stanford fans still disagree), and the only penalty was on Stanford, for too many players on the field. Cal had a touchdown and the win, and The Play became the craziest sequence of events in the history of sports.

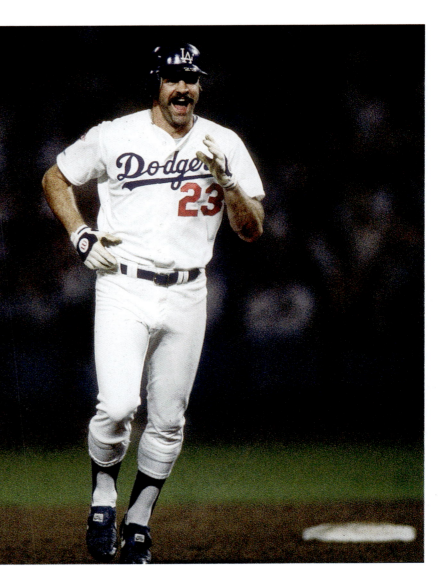

2 Dodgers vs. A's: Kirk Gibson's World Series walk-off home run
October 15, 1988

It was Game 1 of the 1988 World Series, and the Los Angeles Dodgers were without their best hitter. Veteran outfielder Kirk Gibson had injured his left hamstring and right knee during the National League Championship Series and could barely walk, let alone play in the game. He didn't make it out to the dugout and didn't even put on his uniform. But trailing 4–3 with two outs and a runner on base in the bottom of the ninth, and with star closer Dennis Eckersley on the mound for the Oakland A's, L.A. needed a hero. After Gibson took some swings off a tee in the clubhouse, manager Tommy Lasorda called him out to pinch-hit. Gibson limped out to the plate. He fouled off three pitches on the way to working a full count. Eckersley then unleashed his devastating slider, down and in, but Gibson wasn't fooled: He launched it over the right-centerfield wall. Gibson slowly limped around the bases, pumping his fists, as the underdog Dodgers had a Game 1 upset. They went on to win the Series in five games.

3 Steelers vs. Raiders: The Immaculate Reception
December 23, 1972

It looked as if the Oakland Raiders were going to get the best of the Pittsburgh Steelers in the AFC divisional playoff game. The Steelers trailed 7–6 and faced a fourth-and-10 at their own 40 with 22 seconds left. Under pressure, quarterback Terry Bradshaw scrambled and heaved a prayer downfield toward running back John Fuqua. Raiders safety Jack Tatum leveled Fuqua at the Raiders' 33 as the ball arrived, and the ball bounced back about 10 yards. Running back Franco Harris *(right)* was at the right place at the right time. He caught the ball just before it hit the ground and took off down the left side, stiff-arming Jimmy Warren before tight-roping down the final five yards into the end zone. If the ball had hit only Fuqua, it would have been an illegal reception and the Raiders would have won. But the officials confirmed that the ball hit Fuqua *and* Tatum, so the Steelers had the touchdown and the win.

4 Yankees vs. Cubs: Babe Ruth's called shot
October 1, 1932

This was Babe Ruth's most famous of his home runs — and also the most controversial. It was Game 3 of the 1932 World Series, and the New York Yankees and Chicago Cubs were tied 4–4 in the fifth inning. With a 2–2 count, Ruth stepped out of the batter's box and seemed to point toward centerfield. Some believe he was calling his shot, while others say he was pointing at pitcher Charlie Root, who had "quick-pitched" Ruth before he was ready. There's no clear footage of it, but one thing is for sure: Ruth blasted the next pitch far past the centerfield wall, nearly 500 feet. It's still one of the longest hits in the history of Wrigley Field.

7 Boston College vs. Miami: Doug Flutie's Hail Mary
November 23, 1984

Boston College QB Doug Flutie wasn't your typical passer. He was only 5' 7" and wore uniform number 22, making him look even more like a small running back. BC was on the road facing Miami, and the two teams played an amazing shootout. BC jumped out to an early 14–0 lead after the first quarter and was up 21–15 at halftime. Miami came storming back, and the 'Canes took a 45–41 lead with 28 seconds left. Flutie had moved his Eagles to Miami's 48-yard line in time for one final play. But there was a stiff wind blowing in Flutie's face, and Miami's defensive backs didn't think the tiny quarterback's throw would reach the end zone, especially after he was chased back to his own side. But Flutie launched a perfect spiral, overthrowing the Miami defense as the ball landed in the arms of receiver Gerard Phelan. The Hail Mary catch gave BC one of the most memorable wins in football history.

8 Titans vs. Bills: Music City Miracle
January 8, 2000

The Tennessee Titans pulled off a play for the ages against the Buffalo Bills in a wild-card playoff game. Buffalo was kicking off after taking a 16–15 lead with 14 seconds left. Bills kicker Steve Christie popped up a short kick that Titans fullback Lorenzo Neal caught at the 24. Neal was a great blocker but never much of a running threat. He took a few steps to the right and handed it back to tight end Frank Wycheck, also not much of a runner. Wycheck headed right, drawing tacklers his way, then turned and threw a line-drive pass straight across the field to wide receiver Kevin Dyson. With a string of blockers walling off the left side of the field, Dyson ran 75 yards untouched into the end zone. Many in Buffalo still claim that Wycheck's lateral was a forward pass, but the play was upheld on review, and the Titans' Music City Miracle gave them a stunning 22–16 victory.

5 Giants vs. Patriots: The helmet catch at Super Bowl XLII
February 3, 2008

David Tyree was struggling with drops in the week of practice leading up to Super Bowl XLII, so it was surprising that the special-teams ace was even on the field on offense as the New York Giants tried to upset the undefeated New England Patriots. Trailing 14–10 with 1:15 left, the Giants faced a third-and-five at their own 44-yard line. Quarterback Eli Manning dropped back and was quickly swarmed by pass rushers and looked sure to be sacked. But with Patriots defensive end Jarvis Green grabbing on to Manning's shoulder pads, Manning managed to spin out of the sack. He reset 10 yards behind the line of scrimmage and threw a prayer down the middle of the field. Tyree went up for the ball along with Patriots safety Rodney Harrison, who also had a hand on the ball. Tyree pinned the ball against his helmet with his right hand and kept it there as he crashed to the ground at the 24. It was the most amazing catch in Super Bowl history. Four plays later, Manning connected with Plaxico Burress for a touchdown pass with 35 seconds left, sealing the Super Bowl upset.

6 1996 Olympics: Kerri Strug's gold medal landing
July 23, 1996

At the 1996 Olympic Games in Atlanta, everything was going right for the U.S. team, which was in position to knock off powerhouse Russia to win the country's first women's gymnastics team gold medal. But with a chance to clinch gold on the vault, the U.S. struggled. Strug, who was last up, landed awkwardly on her first attempt, injuring her ankle. Team USA needed Strug to land her second attempt, but she could barely walk. Coach Bela Karolyi famously urged her on, telling her, "You can do it!" Strug took off and landed her second vault, hopping on her one good foot as she saluted the judges before falling to her knees. The courageous vault scored a 9.712, enough to clinch the gold. (Karolyi had to carry her to the medal podium.) Afterward, it was discovered that she had a third-degree sprain (the most severe) as well as tendon damage in her ankle.

9 Jimmy Connors vs. Guillermo Vilas: Connors's racket in the air
February 23, 1996

Tennis legend Jimmy Connors had many memorable moments throughout his Hall of Fame career, but his craziest point came on the seniors' tour. During a match at the Corel Champions Tournament, Connors was playing close to the net, so his opponent, Guillermo Vilas, tried to lob the ball over his head. Instead of sprinting back to get the ball, Connors threw his racket straight up into the air. His timing was perfect: The face of his racket made contact with the ball in midair, resulting in a perfectly placed drop shot. Connors caught the racket and celebrated, but unfortunately the chair umpire ruled the remarkable shot illegal.

10 Boise State vs. Oklahoma: Statue of Liberty play
January 1, 2007

There have been a few college football teams labeled "BCS busters," smaller schools that have held their own with the big boys. The most famous is Boise State, the school from Idaho that's always in the hunt for a major bowl berth. In 2007, the Broncos made the Fiesta Bowl, where they faced heavily favored Oklahoma. Boise hung tough all day. Down seven with 18 seconds left and facing a fourth-and-18, the Broncos ran a hook-and-lateral (a trick play in which the receiver catches the ball and then laterals to another player) to tie the score and force overtime. In OT, Oklahoma got the ball first and put up seven points, but Boise had more tricks up its sleeve. First they scored with receiver Vinny Perretta lined up at QB and flipping a pass to Derek Schouman. Instead of tying it with the extra point, Boise went for two. Quarterback Jared Zabransky dropped back and faked a throw right. He then handed it off behind his back to star running back Ian Johnson *(left)*. The entire OU defense was fooled by the play, known as the Statue of Liberty, and Johnson scored to give Boise a 43–42 victory.

1 Nolan Ryan
MLB pitcher, Career: 1966–93

In 1974, Ryan's fastball was clocked at 100.9 miles per hour, but the way pitches were measured in the 1970s underestimated the speed of the ball. Some experts believe Ryan's heater actually traveled 108.1 mph. While not every pitch was quite that fast, Ryan's fastball was the greatest of all time. He has the Ks to prove it. The Ryan Express totaled 5,714 strikeouts, the most in baseball history, over a 27-year career.

2 Eddie Feigner
Softball pitcher, Career: 1946–2000

For more than 50 years, the best fast-pitch softball pitcher *ever* traveled the U.S., taking on all comers. Feigner's team, called The King and His Court, had only four players because he rarely let anyone get a bat on the ball. Feigner threw pitches blindfolded, between his legs, behind his back, and even from centerfield. In a charity game, he once faced legends Willie Mays, Maury Wills, Roberto Clemente, Brooks Robinson, Willie McCovey, and Harmon Killebrew — and struck them all out in a row. His fastball was regularly clocked above 100 miles per hour, and some claim he still threw a 112-mph heater after he turned 40.

Top 10 Stron

6 Shoaib Akhtar
Cricket bowler, Career: 1997–2007

In the modern era of cricket, no one can match the pure power of Akhtar. The bowler from Pakistan is one of only three bowlers in cricket history to have broken the 100-mile-per-hour barrier. During the 2003 World Cup against England he unleashed a 100.3-mph throw, the fastest ever recorded.

7 Aroldis Chapman
MLB pitcher, Career: 2010–present

The Cincinnati Reds lefty fireballer is the hardest thrower in today's game. Chapman owns the fastest pitch ever recorded by Pitch f/x, the most accurate program for measuring pitch speeds. As a rookie in September 2010, he blew a fastball past Tony Gwynn Jr. that was recorded at 105.1 miles per hour. In his first 19 career pitches, his heater averaged 101.3 mph.

8 Yukiko Ueno
Softball pitcher, Career: 2001–present

The U.S. dominated Olympic softball until Japan's Ueno came along. With a 75-mile-per-hour pitch, she is the hardest thrower in her sport. In 2004, she threw the first-ever perfect game in Olympic history. At the 2008 Games, she led underdog Japan to a gold medal. A day after losing to the U.S. in a 10-inning game, Ueno first beat Australia, and then, after an hour of rest, defeated the U.S. In all, she threw 28 innings in two days to help Japan take home gold.

3 Steve Dalkowski
Minor league pitcher, Career: 1957–65

Dalkowski might have had the fastest pitch in baseball history, yet he never made it to the big leagues. That's because he never knew where his fastballs would end up. In a nine-year minor league career, he struck out a whopping 1,396 batters in 995 innings . . . and walked 1,354. He was rumored to have thrown well over 105 miles per hour.

4 John Elway
NFL quarterback, Career: 1983–98

At 6'3" and about 200 pounds with skinny arms, Elway wasn't the biggest guy, but no quarterback has ever thrown with more velocity than the Denver Broncos Hall of Famer. In fact, his receivers had lasting reminders of how powerfully Elway fired the ball. Tattooed on their chest was the Elway Cross, a bruise caused by the tip of the football hitting them.

5 Satchel Paige
Negro Leagues and MLB pitcher, Career: 1926–53, '65

While most hurlers have at least two different pitches, Paige pretty much threw *only* a fastball — though he did give his one pitch slight variations and different names. (There was Long Tommy, Bat Dodger, Be Ball, and Midnight Rider.) Because of racial segregation, Paige didn't make his major league debut until age 42. But even then he was throwing heat past big league hitters. Over six years in the bigs, he had 288 Ks in 476 innings and a 3.29 ERA.

gest Arms

9 Brett Favre
NFL quarterback, Career: 1991–2010

Favre earned a reputation as a gunslinger, a player who was totally unpredictable in his decisions and was willing to throw passes anywhere, no matter what the defense did. Favre got away with that mentality because he threw the ball so hard. How hard? Just ask Antonio Freeman, Favre's go-to receiver on the Green Bay Packers from the mid-1990s through the early 2000s. Freeman says Favre's passes either sprained or dislocated seven of his 10 fingers over the years.

10 Walter Johnson
MLB pitcher, Career: 1907–27

As legend has it, after big leaguer Cliff Blankenship saw Johnson pitch on a scouting trip, his report on the future Hall of Famer's fastball was "You can't hit what you can't see." In 1917, the Bridgeport munitions laboratory timed baseball's hardest throwers — Johnson, Smokey Joe Wood, and Christy Mathewson — to see how far their throws traveled in one second. The results: Wood, 124 feet; Mathewson, 127; and Johnson, 134.

TOP 10 SPORTS MOVIES

Hoosiers

This feel-good basketball tale is loosely based on the 1954 Indiana state high school basketball championship. Seeing a tiny hoops-crazed town learn to rally around the team led by a hard-nosed coach is inspiring. *Hoosiers* showcases the David-versus-Goliath spirit that all the best sports movies have.

2 Rocky
The 1976 Oscar winner for best picture tells the story of struggling Philadelphia boxer Rocky Balboa. Underdogs everywhere will pump their fists watching a gutsy Rocky battle champion prize-fighter Apollo Creed in a high-stakes showdown. Rocky's infectious never-give-up attitude packs a mean punch.

3 Remember the Titans
Based on a true story of the integration of Virginia's T.C. Williams High School football team, the Titans must come together to achieve championship glory. It isn't easy, but the Titans define what being a team is all about.

4 Hoop Dreams
Facing poverty and inner-city violence, two high school basketball players have the odds stacked against them. The eye-opening documentary reveals how the teens rise up against their circumstances for a shot at college scholarships and a better life.

5 A League of Their Own
This World War II–era comedy tells the story of the trailblazers who created the first female professional baseball league. Dugout jokes keep the film lighthearted, but highlighting female baseball pioneers makes it powerful.

6 Rudy
His small size, poor grades, and lack of money threaten to keep Rudy from playing for the Notre Dame Fighting Irish. However, Rudy's steadfast determination not only leads him to the Notre Dame gridiron as a walk-on, but also shows us that heroes come in all sizes.

7 Seabiscuit
An unlikely champion racehorse lifts the spirits of a nation during the Great Depression in this Oscar-nominated drama. With the help of trainers, the undersized Seabiscuit becomes a legendary thoroughbred.

8 Chariots of Fire
Two British track athletes from different backgrounds — one is a Christian Scotsman, the other is a Jewish Englishman — clash as competitors at Cambridge and become teammates at the 1924 Olympics. *Chariots of Fire* is a story of staying true to one's beliefs when victory is on the line.

9 The Natural
In this mythical tale, a bat carved out of wood from a lightning-struck tree propels an unknown middle-aged batter named Roy Hobbs to baseball stardom. Hobbs becomes a legend and shows us anything is possible.

10 The Mighty Ducks
The lesson: A second chance doesn't come often, but when it does, take it. A lawyer who is haunted by childhood memories of not making the winning goal in a shootout is redeemed while coaching a group of youngsters against his old squad.

TOP 10 F

1 The Mannings
Eli, Peyton, and Archie; Football
The first family of quarterbacks includes dad Archie, a star at Ole Miss before leading the New Orleans Saints. Middle son Peyton is one of the greatest QBs in NFL history, setting numerous records and guiding the Indianapolis Colts to a Super Bowl XLI win. And youngest son Eli has topped his dad and older brother with two Super Bowl rings with the New York Giants.

2 The Griffeys
Ken Jr. and Ken Sr.; Baseball
Ken Sr. was a solid hitter and three-time All-Star. Ken Jr., who displayed power at the plate and acrobatics in the field, is a surefire Hall of Famer. The two were briefly teammates on the Seattle Mariners. On September 14, 1990, Senior homered to left centerfield. Then Junior followed up with a blast to almost the same spot to become MLB's first father-son duo to hit back-to-back homers.

3 The Earnhardts
Dale Sr. and Dale Jr.; Auto Racing
Dale Sr. was "The Intimidator," a supremely talented and very aggressive driver who won seven titles in NASCAR's highest circuit (tied with Richard Petty for the most of all time). His Number 3 remains one of the most popular symbols of NASCAR. His son, Dale Jr., has been a fan favorite, winning the Sprint Cup Series Most Popular Driver award every year from 2003 to '12.

4 The Howes
Marty, Gordie, and Mark; Hockey
Known as "Mr. Hockey," Gordie Howe is an all-time great and one of two NHL players with 800 career goals. (Wayne Gretzky is the other.) Gordie suited up with sons Mark and Marty for the WHA's Houston Aeros and New England Whalers and the NHL's Hartford Whalers. Mark joined his father in the Hall of Fame in 2011, and Marty had a respectable 12-year career.

5 The Ripkens
Cal Jr., Cal Sr., and Billy; Baseball
In 1987, Cal Sr. was the Baltimore Orioles' manager. Oldest son Cal Jr. was the team's star shortstop, having won the American League MVP in 1983 while leading the O's to a World Series title. Younger brother Billy joined them in July that season, hitting .308 as a utility infielder. Cal Jr. and Billy now run their own youth baseball organization under the family name.

AMILIES

6 The Matthewses
Clay III, Bruce, and Clay Jr.; Football

With his long blond locks, Green Bay Packers star pass rusher Clay III might be the most recognizable Matthews. But his dad, Clay Jr., was a four-time Pro Bowl linebacker during his playing days. Bruce, the brother of Clay Jr. and uncle of Clay III, might be the best of them all. He's in the Hall of Fame for his accomplishments as an offensive lineman.

7 The Pettys
Kyle, Adam, Richard, and Lee; Auto Racing

The Pettys made their mark in the sport over four generations. Lee had a Hall of Fame career that included a win at the first Daytona 500 in 1959. His son Richard is a legend whose 200 wins are 95 more than anyone else has won. Richard's son, Kyle, has won eight Sprint Cup races. Kyle's son Adam was a promising young driver who tragically died while practicing for a race.

8 The Sutters
Ron, Rich, Brent, Duane, Brian, and Darryl; Hockey

It seems like the NHL has always had a Sutter. That's because six Sutter brothers played in the league, with careers spanning parts of four decades. As players, they collectively have 1,320 regular-season goals and six Stanley Cups. (Duane has won four and Brent has two.) Darryl also won a Cup as coach of the Los Angeles Kings in 2011–12.

9 The Barrys
Rick and Brent; Basketball

The Barry family sure can shoot. Rick is a Hall of Famer famous for underhand free throws and a 90 percent career free-throw mark. Three of his sons — Brent, Jon, and Drew — played in the NBA. Brent had the most noteworthy career. He was the champion of the 1996 Slam Dunk Contest before becoming a three-point specialist and winning two titles with the San Antonio Spurs.

10 The Granatos
Tony and Cammi; Hockey

Tony spent 13 seasons in the NHL, a respected veteran who played in the 1997 All-Star Game. But he's got nothing on his little sister, Cammi, who is in the Hockey Hall of Fame as one of the greatest women's players of all time. As captain of the U.S. team that won gold at the 1998 Olympics, she scored the first goal in USA women's hockey Olympic history.

Top 10 Controversial Calls

1 Seahawks vs. Packers
September 24, 2012

NFL replacement refs were responsible for the most controversial call in recent memory. As time expired on a *Monday Night Football* game, Packers safety M.D. Jennings appeared to intercept the Seahawks' Hail Mary in the end zone before Seattle wide receiver Golden Tate wrestled to claim possession. The inexperienced refs contradicted each other's call on the field. They eventually incorrectly ruled it a Seattle touchdown, gifting the Seahawks a 14–12 victory. The call was so heavily criticized that it effectively ended the referee lockout, bringing the regular officials back.

2 Royals vs. Cardinals
October 26, 1985

Up 1–0 in the bottom of the ninth inning of Game 6 of the World Series, St. Louis was three outs from a title. Kansas City's Jorge Orta led off the inning with a slow roller to first. Pitcher Todd Worrell covered the base and Jack Clark's throw beat Orta by a half step. But not to umpire Don Denkinger. He called the runner safe despite the protests of the Cardinals. St. Louis unraveled after the call, misplaying a routine pop-up and allowing a passed ball. The Royals scored two runs, forced a Game 7, and won the World Series.

3 United States vs. USSR
September 9, 1972

With one second left in the 1972 Olympic gold medal men's basketball game and the U.S. ahead by one point, the USSR seemingly had one last inbound play. But a series of protests by the Soviets and referee errors resulted in the USSR getting *three* chances to inbound the ball. On their third try, the Soviets scored a winning basket at the buzzer, stealing the game and Olympic gold. The Americans, who thought they had won after the first redo, were so upset that they didn't attend the medal ceremony and have never accepted their silvers.

4 England vs. Argentina
June 22, 1986

One of the World Cup's most famous goals shouldn't have counted. Argentina's star Diego Maradona had snuck behind England's defense. He leaped, but instead of heading the ball, he punched it in the goal with his hand. It was a clear handball to everyone but the referee. Argentina went on to win the quarterfinal match 2–1. After the match, Maradona famously said it was "the hand of God" that put the ball in the net.

5 Colorado vs. Missouri
October 6, 1990

With 30 seconds left, the Colorado football team was trailing Missouri 31–27 and had first-and-goal on the four. Over the next four downs, they spiked the ball, got stuffed twice, and, on fourth down, spiked the ball again. That should've ended the game, but the refs and the chain crew had lost track and gave the Buffs a fifth down. That's when they scored and won the game. The Big 8 Conference suspended seven officials for the bad call.

6 Orioles vs. Yankees
October 9, 1996

With the O's up by one in Game 1 of the AL Championship Series, the Yankees' Derek Jeter hit a deep fly in the eighth inning. Outfielder Tony Tarasco parked under the ball when a young fan named Jeffrey Maier suddenly reached out with his glove and knocked it away. Though it was interference, the umpire called it a home run. The solo shot tied the game, and New York went on to win the game and later the series.

7 Sabres vs. Stars
June 19, 1999

It was triple overtime of Game 6 of the Stanley Cup finals. The Stars' Brett Hull scrambled in front of the Buffalo net, gained control of the puck, and slid it past goalie Dominik Hasek, clinching the Cup for Dallas. What angered Buffalo was that Hull's skate was in the crease as he took his shot, meaning that it could have been disallowed. The NHL ruled that Hull hadn't lost possession, so his skate could be in the crease.

8 Jets vs. Seahawks
December 6, 1998

The NFL started using instant replay largely because of this play. The Seahawks tackled Jets quarterback Vinny Testaverde at the one-yard line on fourth down at the end of the game. But officials mistook his helmet for the football and ruled that he had crossed the goal line, giving New York a 32–31 win. The phantom touchdown caused Seattle to go 8–8 and miss the playoffs.

9 Tigers vs. Indians
June 2, 2010

Through the 2012 season, 23 pitchers in MLB history had thrown a perfect game. It should be 24. In a game against the Indians, Tigers pitcher Armando Galarraga was one out away from a perfect game. On the 27th batter, he covered first on a grounder. The throw beat the runner by half a step. However, umpire Jim Joyce called him safe, costing the pitcher a place in the record books. Joyce later apologized for the blown call.

10 Canada vs. Russia
February 11, 2002

At the Salt Lake City Olympics, Canadian figure skating pair Jamie Salé and David Pelletier had the performance of their lives. The judges disagreed and gave the Russian team the gold and the Canadians the silver. Amid public outcry, a French judge admitted that her federation had pressured her to ensure the Russians won. Within a week, the Canadians were awarded a gold medal too.

Top 10 Logos

1 New York Yankees

The most famous logo in sports also has a proud backstory. The interlocking NY logo first appeared on a medal given to officer John McDowell, the first New York City police officer shot in the line of duty. The New York Highlanders (who later became the Yankees) started wearing the logo on their caps and left sleeves, in part because one of the club's owners, Bill Devery, was a former New York City police chief.

2 Boston Celtics

Legendary Boston Celtics coach Red Auerbach was not the only member of his family to play a big part in the team's legacy. His brother, Zang, designed the Celtics logo in the 1950s, creating a winking leprechaun who had the perfect amount of confidence to represent the greatest franchise in pro basketball. The Celtics officially adopted it as their logo in 1968.

3 Dallas Cowboys

Jack Eskridge, the equipment manager under legendary Dallas coach Tom Landry, came up with the famous blue star for the Cowboys' first season in 1960. That star, representing the Lone Star State, is also prominently displayed in the midfield of Cowboys Stadium.

4 Texas Longhorns

The University of Texas's burnt-orange Longhorn has become the most famous symbol in college football. In the early 1900s, Texas's teams were commonly known as the Varsity or Steers, but the current name caught on in 1913, when a booster donated blankets emblazoned with TEXAS LONGHORNS. The Longhorn head logo made its debut in 1961.

5 Milwaukee Brewers

In 1977, the Brewers held a contest for fans to design a new logo. Art history student Tom Meindel won the $2,000 prize with a unique and creative entry: a lowercase M served as the fingers on a baseball glove, while the letter B formed the mitt and thumb. The Brewers changed their look in 1994, but the classic logo still shows up on throwback days.

6 Montreal Canadiens

The Canadiens' record 24 Stanley Cup titles have helped make their logo iconic. Many think the letter H within the C stands for *Habs*, the team's nickname. (*Les Habitants* were the original French settlers in Quebec.) It actually stands for *hockey*. In 1916–17, when the logo first appeared, the team was known as *Club de Hockey Canadien*.

7 Chicago Bulls

Even if Michael Jordan had never donned a Bulls uniform or led Chicago to six NBA championships, its logo would still be one of the fiercest in sports. With a furrowed brow and sharp horns, the Bull hasn't changed since the franchise's first season in 1966–67.

8 Hartford Whalers

Being one of the hottest-selling logos in your sport means that you have a pretty good design. Being one of the hottest-selling logos in sports 16 years after your team played its last game means that you have one of the greatest ever. The Whalers' logo features a W combined with a whale's tail, forming a white H for *Hartford* in the middle. Even though the NHL franchise moved to Carolina after the 1996–97 season, the Whalers remain among the top five best-selling teams for the sports apparel company Mitchell & Ness.

9 Manchester United

For the majority of its existence, Manchester United was known as the Reds or simply United. In 1973, legendary manager Matt Busby watched a local rugby club, the Salfold City Reds, tour France. He took a liking to their intimidating red-devil logo. Busby adopted the logo for his own team and Man U. became the Red Devils.

10 Pittsburgh Steelers

In 1962, the Steelers were looking for a design for their helmets. A company in Cleveland called Republic Steel suggested that the team use the Steelmark logo. Unsure of how it would look, the team put it on only one side of its helmets. Pittsburgh went on to enjoy one of its best seasons to date and decided the logo was good luck (and so was using it on only one side). With the steel industry being so big in its hometown, the team and its logo have been a perfect match.

1

Michael Jordan
NBA guard,
Career: 1984–93, '95–98, 2001–03

Jordan is considered by many to be the greatest basketball player ever to have lived. MJ didn't score the most points, or win the most titles or MVP awards, but he single-handedly dominated both ends of the court like no other player in the history of the NBA. His skills and style fundamentally changed the game of basketball.

Top 10 Greatest

Athletes

2 Muhammad Ali
Boxer, Career: 1960–81

Known as The Greatest, Ali virtually invented the art of trash talking. But he backed it up, winning the world heavyweight title three times. Ali's character, charisma, and athletic dominance made a lasting impact on superstars across all sports.

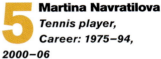

3 **Wayne Gretzky**
NHL center, Career: 1979–99
His nickname said it all: The Great One. Gretzky is unquestionably the greatest hockey player of all time. When he retired, he held 61 NHL records. He is the only player to amass 200 points in a single season, something he did four times.

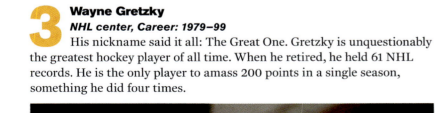

4 **Jim Thorpe**
Track and field star, MLB outfielder, and NFL halfback; Career: 1912–29
Thorpe is the greatest three-sport star ever. He won Olympic medals in the decathlon and pentathlon in 1912. After his Olympic triumph, he had a career as a professional baseball and football player until he was in his 40s. THE GREATEST ATHLETE IN THE WORLD is written on his tombstone.

5 **Martina Navratilova**
Tennis player, Career: 1975–94, 2000–06
No tennis player was as great for as long a time as Navratilova. She won a record 59 Grand Slam titles — 18 singles, 31 doubles, and 10 mixed doubles — during her professional career. She is also one of three women to complete the Grand Slam "boxed set," winning the slam in singles, doubles, and mixed doubles.

6 Jim Brown
Lacrosse midfielder and NFL fullback; Career: 1954–65

Despite being best known for his football skills, Brown is more than a gridiron legend. At Syracuse University, he was an All-America lacrosse player and averaged more than 10 points per game for the basketball team, all while starring in football. His NFL career was most impressive. When he retired, he held career records for rushing yards and touchdowns.

7 Michael Phelps
Olympic swimmer, Career: 2000–12

Phelps was the most dominant swimmer in the history of the sport. He took home 18 gold medals, twice as many as anyone else in history, over three Olympics. His 22 overall medals are also a record. Phelps will always be remembered for his eight-gold-medal performance at the 2008 Beijing Games, the most any athlete has ever won in a single Olympics.

9 Babe Didrikson Zaharias
Track and field star and golfer; Career: 1930–55

Didrikson Zaharias was already an All-America basketball player and a track and field national champion when she took up the game of golf in 1934. And she had the same kind of success she had in her other sports. She won the U.S. Women's Amateur in 1946 and became the first American to win the British Ladies Amateur in 1947. By 1950 she had won every golf title in existence, amateur and professional.

8 Babe Ruth
MLB outfielder,
Career: 1914–35

The Babe left an indelible mark on baseball, converting it from small ball to the power-hitting game it is today. When he retired, he held dozens of single-season and career batting records. But he wasn't a one-dimensional slugger. Early in his career, he was a star pitcher, amassing a 3–0 record in the World Series for the Boston Red Sox.

10 Mia Hamm
Soccer forward,
Career: 1987–2004

Hamm helped bring women's soccer to prominence. At the time of her retirement, Hamm's 158 international goals in 275 games were more than any other person, male or female, had scored in soccer history. She was also part of the nearly unbeatable University of North Carolina dynasty that won four national titles.

TOP 10 LITTLE

Height: 5' 7"	Weight: 148 lbs

1 Lionel Messi
Soccer forward

Messi is nicknamed the Atomic Flea. Indeed, the Argentinian soccer star plays like a tiny pest — he darts around the field, changing direction on a dime, and he has the skills to score from almost anywhere. Despite his size, Messi has won four straight Ballon d'Or awards (2009 through '12), which is given to the world's best soccer player.

Height: 5' 3"	Weight: 141 lbs

2 Muggsy Bogues
NBA point guard

As the shortest player in NBA history, Bogues looked like a little sapling among tall trees on the court. But what he lacked in height he made up for with lightning-quick speed, deft ball handling, and quality passing. In 1999–2000, he showed his skills as a floor general for the Toronto Raptors by leading the league with an impressive 5.07 assist-to-turnover ratio.

Height: 5' 4"	Weight: 140 lbs

3 Willie Keeler
MLB outfielder

Because of his stature, Keeler was known as Wee Willie, but there was nothing small about his bat. Keeler had eight 200-hit seasons, and in 1898, he smacked 206 singles alone, a record that stood for more than 100 years. One of the shortest players in the Hall of Fame, Keeler holds the National League mark for consecutive games with a hit (45).

Height: 4' 11"	Weight: 130 lbs

4 Naim Suleymanoglu
Weightlifter

Nicknamed Pocket Hercules, Suleymanoglu began building his legend early in life. At just 15 years old, he set his first world record. A year later, he lifted three times his own bodyweight, something that had been done by only one other man. Suleymanoglu became the first man in weightlifting history to win three straight Olympic gold medals (1988, '92, '96).

Height: 5' 5"	Weight: 152 lbs

5 Diego Maradona
Soccer midfielder

Maradona captained Argentina's national soccer team to the 1986 World Cup title. He was a virtuoso with the ball at his feet, and scored what many consider the greatest goal in soccer history. In the 1986 World Cup quarterfinals, Maradona dribbled 60 yards through England's defense, weaving down the field, before hitting the back of the net.

GUYS

Height: 5'7"	Weight: 210 lbs

6 Maurice Jones-Drew
NFL running back

You could call Jones-Drew short, but he's certainly not small. Jones-Drew's body and legs are so compact and powerful that he appears to be as wide as he is tall. Through the 2012 season, the Jacksonville Jaguars rusher had run for 7,268 career yards, averaging 4.6 yards per carry. His 76 touchdowns from 2006 through '12 are the third most in the NFL during that span.

Height: 5'5"	Weight: 137 lbs

7 Sachin Tendulkar
Cricketer

Regarded as one of the greatest to ever play cricket, Tendulkar has gathered batting records in his sport the way Wayne Gretzky set scoring standards in hockey. Playing for the Indian national team, Tendulkar tallied the most runs in test cricket history. He was the first to score 100 runs 100 times in international appearances, a mark no one else has come close to.

Height: 5'10"	Weight: 180 lbs

8 Doug Flutie
NFL quarterback

Flutie, a Heisman Trophy winner, was deemed too small to play in the NFL, so in 1990 he took his aggressive style to the Canadian Football League, winning three CFL titles. In 2006, Canadian sports network TSN named him the Number 1 CFL player of all time. After so much success up north, he signed with the Buffalo Bills, leading them to the playoffs in 1998 and '99.

Height: 5'8"	Weight: 165 lbs

9 Dustin Pedroia
MLB second baseman

The diminutive Red Sox star has always come up big at the plate. In 2008 he won a Silver Slugger award as the American League's top-hitting second baseman and was named the AL MVP after leading the league in hits (213), doubles (54), and runs scored (118). Pedroia's size also does not diminish his range in the field: He won Gold Glove awards in '08 and '11.

Height: 5'6"	Weight: 182 lbs

10 Theo Fleury
NHL right wing

When the Calgary Flames called up Fleury during the 1988–89 season, it turned their year around. He had five goals and six assists during that postseason, helping Calgary win the Stanley Cup. Fleury went on to become a seven-time All-Star. He finished among the top 10 in goals and points three times during his career, despite usually being the shortest guy on the ice.

TOP 10
BIG GUYS

1

Height: 7'1"   Weight: 325 lbs

Shaquille O'Neal
NBA center

In his prime, Shaq was the most dominant force in the NBA. He was so big and strong, the only way to stop him was through "hack-a-Shaq." That's when teams fouled O'Neal as hard as they could so that he couldn't make a basket and had to take free throws instead, the only part of the game in which he struggled. The 15-time NBA All-Star's career peaked during his 1999–2000 MVP season with the Los Angeles Lakers, when he led the NBA in scoring with 29.7 points per game. That year he won the first of four titles and first of three NBA Finals MVP awards.

Height: 7'1"   Weight: 270 lbs

2   Wilt Chamberlain
NBA center

Considered one of the greatest basketball players of all time, Chamberlain towered over the NBA. Wilt the Stilt took home MVP honors four times, became the only NBA player to score 100 points in a game, set the record for most rebounds in league history (23,924), and won the scoring title seven straight years. As a testament to his control over his 7'1" frame, Chamberlain didn't foul out once in 1,205 regular-season and playoff games.

4 Randy Johnson
MLB pitcher
The Big Unit is the tallest pitcher ever to play in the big leagues. During his career from 1988 through 2009, he struck out nearly 1,000 more batters than any other pitcher over that span.

5 B.J. Raji
NFL nose tackle
Raji excels at gobbling up offensive linemen, who have to double team the big Green Bay Packers Pro Bowler to keep him at bay. This gives his linebackers the ability to cause havoc. When he scored a TD in the 2010 playoffs, he did a belly-jiggling shimmy that made him famous.

3 Akebono Taro
Sumo wrestler
Weighing in at a quarter of a ton, Taro was big even in the sport of sumo, where huge is the norm. In 1993 he made history by rising to the rank of Yokozuna, which is the highest honor for a sumo wrestler. The Hawaiian was the first non-Japanese-born wrestler to achieve the feat. He maintained his vaunted ranking for eight years until his retirement.

Height: 6' 7" **Weight: 290 lbs**

6 CC Sabathia
MLB pitcher

You could easily confuse the star pitcher for an NFL left tackle. But when you see Sabathia on the mound, you know he's in the right place. The 2007 AL Cy Young winner uses a power-pitching arsenal to make opponents whiff. He ranked in the top 10 in strikeouts in 10 of his first 12 seasons and led the league in wins twice.

Height: 7' 2" **Weight: 225 lbs**

7 Kareem Abdul-Jabbar
NBA center

No one has sunk more buckets in the history of the NBA than Abdul-Jabbar, the league's all-time leading scorer (38,387 points). The lean and lanky Abdul-Jabbar used his polished offensive game to devastating effect, scoring regularly with his signature skyhook. When Abdul-Jabbar retired, he held the career record for blocks, since eclipsed by Dikembe Mutombo and Hakeem Olajuwon. However, Abdul-Jabbar still has more MVP awards (six) and NBA titles (six) than Mutombo and Olajuwon combined.

Height: 7' 6" **Weight: 310 lbs**

9 Yao Ming
NBA center

This gentle giant had his career cut short by injuries, but he accomplished a great deal. He made eight All-Star teams and five All-NBA teams. He used his size to guard the paint for the Houston Rockets, twice finishing in the top 10 in blocks. Yao didn't only have size — he also possessed great basketball skills. He shot 52 percent from the field and 83 percent from the line in his career. Yao also helped grow the game in his native China, and remains an international superstar.

Height: 6' 9" **Weight: 255 lbs**

8 Zdeno Chara
NHL defenseman

The Boston Bruins' big captain, Chara is the tallest player in a league where the average skater is 6'1". The defenseman uses that size to his advantage. Known for punishing hits and a huge slap shot, Chara is a five-time winner of the hardest-shot event at the NHL All-Star Skills Competition.

Height: 6' 2" **Weight: 335 lbs**

10 William Perry
NFL defensive lineman

In today's NFL, 335 pounds is big, but certainly not the heaviest in the league. During the 2012 season, 426 players weighed more than 300 pounds. But in 1985, only 23 players were that heavy. The heaviest of them all was Chicago Bears defensive tackle Perry. The Refrigerator was a lovable member of the vaunted '85 Bears defense who also lined up as a fullback and scored a rushing touchdown in Super Bowl XX.

CLUTCH PERFORMA

1 Joe Montana's game-winning drive in the Super Bowl
Super Bowl XXIII, January 22, 1989

There's a reason people called Joe Montana "Joe Cool." In big-pressure situations, he was always in complete control. Montana's calm was on full display in Super Bowl XXIII, when his Niners were down 16–13 to the Cincinnati Bengals with 3:10 left in the game and the ball at their own eight-yard line.

Even with tension running high, Montana kept things light, pointing out to his teammates that the actor John Candy was in the stands. When they broke the huddle, Montana marched the team down the field to the Bengals' 10, calling a timeout with 39 seconds on the clock. On the 11th play of the drive Montana dropped back and threaded a perfect pass between three defenders to hit John Taylor in stride in the end zone, sealing a 20–16 win.

ANCES

2 Christian Laettner's buzzer-beater
NCAA men's basketball tournament, March 28, 1992

Duke forward Christian Laettner couldn't miss a shot. If he had, the Blue Devils would have lost the 1992 East Regional final to Kentucky. He made all 10 free throws and all 10 field goals he took, punctuated by a miracle buzzer-beater that secured a 104–103 victory for the Blue Devils. The underdog Wildcats had taken a one-point lead with 2.1 seconds remaining in overtime and celebrated as if they had won. Duke called a timeout and drew up a play that called for Grant Hill to heave a pass down the court. Hill's Hail Mary connected perfectly to Laettner, who was 75 feet away. Afraid to foul, Kentucky players allowed Laettner to leap and catch the ball just above the free-throw line. Laettner took a dribble, spun, and, just before the buzzer sounded, sank a shot for the ages.

3 **Jesse Owens's four Olympic gold medals in Berlin**
Summer Olympics, August 1936

At the Berlin Olympic Games, American Jesse Owens, 22, stared down opponents on the track and off. Adolf Hitler had risen to power and planned to use the Games as a Nazi propaganda campaign that argued for Aryan racial superiority. In the Nazis' eyes, an African American couldn't compete with Germans. Owens proved how wrong they were. On his way to four gold medals, Owens helped break the world record in the 4 × 100-meter race. He also set Olympic records in the 200 meters and the long jump. His performance at the Games was hailed as the greatest of the century.

4 **Adam Vinatieri's Super Bowl–winning kick**
Super Bowl XXXVI, February 3, 2002

With the game against the St. Louis Rams tied 17–17 and 1:30 left on the clock, Tom Brady marched the Patriots downfield. Then it was all up to Patriots kicker Adam Vinatieri, who would have to make a 48-yard field goal. The snap, hold, and kick were perfect, and the clock expired as the ball split the uprights to secure one of the great upsets in Super Bowl history. Two years later, Vinatieri did it again. Tied 29–29 with the Carolina Panthers, he nailed the game-winning kick from 41 yards to cement his place as the NFL's all-time greatest clutch kicker.

7 **Jack Nicklaus's comeback to win his 20th major**
The Masters, April 13, 1986

As the 1986 Masters approached, journalists thought that legend Jack Nicklaus was over the hill. But the greatest golfer of all time was not done yet. Nicklaus entered the final round in ninth place and was six strokes behind the leader with 10 holes to play. That's when the Golden Bear began his charge. First he sunk three straight birdies. He made an eagle on 15, followed by back-to-back birdies on 16 and 17. When Greg Norman failed to force a playoff, Nicklaus captured his first major in nearly six years and his 20th overall, still a record.

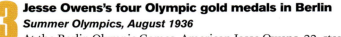

8 **Brandi Chastain's World Cup–winning penalty shot**
World Cup, July 10, 1999

In front of 90,185 people, the U.S. women's soccer team had battled China to a scoreless draw in the final of the Women's World Cup, and the game was coming down to a penalty-kick shootout. With the shootout tied 4–4, Brandi Chastain stepped up to the penalty spot and struck a perfect kick into the side netting. She ripped off her shirt in celebration as her teammates mobbed her, and the U.S. clinched the Cup.

5 **Michael Jordan's title-winning shot**
Game 6 of the NBA Finals, June 14, 1998

The Jazz led the Bulls by three with less than a minute to play in Game 6 of what would be Michael Jordan's last NBA Finals. MJ cut the lead to one with a layup and then stripped Karl Malone on the other end to regain possession. Twelve seconds remained as Jordan took on Utah's Bryon Russell. He drove, nudged Russell out of the way, pulled up, and hit a beautiful jumper that clinched his sixth title.

6 **Mike Eruzione's game-winning goal over the USSR**
Winter Olympics, February 22, 1980

When the U.S. and USSR played in the medal round of the 1980 Olympic hockey tournament, it was a huge mismatch. In an exhibition before the Winter Games, the USSR, the four-time defending Olympic champions, had crushed the U.S. 10–3. At the Olympics, the Soviets dominated early, but the U.S. tied it late in the first period. Down by one halfway through the third period, Mark Johnson tied the score again. Then, 81 seconds later, Team USA captain Mike Eruzione fired a quick wrist shot and scored one of the most famous goals in hockey history. The U.S. hung on to the lead and pulled off the "Miracle on Ice." Two days later the U.S. beat Finland to win the gold medal.

10 **Mary Lou Retton's perfect 10**
Summer Olympics, August 3, 1984

Halfway through the all-around individual final at the 1984 Games, U.S. gymnast Mary Lou Retton found herself neck and neck with favorite Ecaterina Szabo. On the third rotation, Retton scored a perfect 10 on her floor routine to move within .05 points of Szabo with just one event to go. Szabo went first on her apparatus, scoring a 9.9 on the uneven bars, meaning that if Retton scored a 10 on her vault, the gold would be hers. After her coach, Bela Karolyi, gave Retton a dose of encouragement, she took off in a full sprint, launched into the air, and stuck her landing. When the scoreboard flashed a 10.00, fans erupted and Retton celebrated her gold.

9 **Bill Mazeroski's World Series–winning homer**
Game 7 of the World Series, October 13, 1960

Pittsburgh Pirates second baseman Bill Mazeroski won eight Gold Gloves in his 17-year career, but with one swing, his legacy would be defined by a home run. In a tie game going into the bottom of the ninth of Game 7 of the 1960 World Series against the New York Yankees, Maz led off the inning. On a 1–0 count, Yankees pitcher Ralph Terry hung a slider that he slammed more than 406 feet over the leftfield wall to give the underdog Pirates a World Series title and, to date, the only Game 7 World Series walk-off homer.

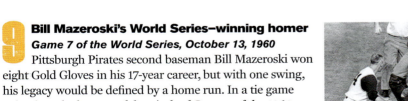

TOP 10 ATHLETE-ACTORS

1 Shaquille O'Neal
NBA center, Career: 1992–2011

On the hardwood, O'Neal dominated the paint. On the big screen, he granted wishes and fought crime. In 1996, the 7'1", 325-pound center transformed into an affable genie in the family film *Kazaam*. The next year he took the lead role in *Steel*, in which he played an armored superhero.

2 Dwayne Johnson
College football defensive tackle, Career: 1991–94

Dwayne Johnson was an intimidating defensive tackle for the 1991 championship-winning Miami Hurricanes and was known in the WWE as the Rock. But on the big screen he showed that he had a softer side in films like 2010's *Tooth Fairy*, putting on tights and wings to play the title role.

3 Chuck Connors
MLB first baseman and NBA forward-center, Career: 1946–51

Connors — one of only 12 athletes to play in both the NBA and MLB, and the first professional basketball player to break a backboard — was a different kind of sharpshooter on TV. He starred as a good-guy cowboy in the TV western series *The Rifleman* and also appeared in 45 movies.

4 Cathy Rigby
Olympic gymnast,
Career: 1968–72

The former U.S. Olympian made good use of her acrobatic skills after she retired from gymnastics, taking flight on Broadway as the boy who wouldn't grow up in *Peter Pan*. She reprised the iconic role several times across the U.S., even as recently as 2013.

5 Merlin Olsen
NFL defensive tackle,
Career: 1962–76

After 15 years as a member of the Fearsome Foursome defensive line for the Los Angeles Rams, the NFL Hall of Famer turned to the small screen and starred in the 1970s show *Little House on the Prairie*. Olsen also appeared in *Father Murphy* and *Aaron's Way*.

6 Jim Brown
NFL fullback,
Career: 1957–65

The NFL Hall of Famer was an all-time great on the gridiron and went on to have a successful acting career. He was a natural in *Any Given Sunday*, playing a football coach in the 1999 flick. He also used his stony demeanor to intimidate martians in the 1996 movie *Mars Attacks!*

7 Alex Karras
NFL defensive tackle, Career: 1958–70

The ferocious All-Pro lineman for the Detroit Lions showed a kinder side in his starring role as an adoptive father in the popular 1980s television series *Webster*. Karras learned his comedic skills from the best — legendary actress Lucille Ball of *I Love Lucy* helped him train for small acting parts when he first got started in showbiz.

8 Johnny Weissmuller
Olympic swimmer, Career: 1921–29

Johnny Weissmuller displayed his upper-body strength in the pool — winning five Olympic gold medals and setting 67 world records in the 1920s — as well as in his second career as the tree-swinging Tarzan. Weissmuller starred as the famous ape man in 20 films throughout the 1930s and '40s.

9 Bob Uecker
MLB catcher, Career: 1962–67

Uecker may have had an unremarkable career on the baseball field, but he became a lovable funny man and a respected broadcaster after retiring. Known for cracking jokes in his role on the 1980s family sitcom *Mr. Belvedere*, the Milwaukee Brewers broadcaster also made dozens of guest appearances on *The Tonight Show*.

10 Fred Dryer
NFL defensive end, Career: 1969–81

Dryer spent 13 years as a menacing NFL defensive end and later became a no-nonsense detective in the 1980s TV drama *Hunter*. He also had a star turn playing a sportscaster on the TV comedy *Cheers*.

TOP 10 JERSEY

1 **Jackie Robinson**
MLB second baseman,
Jersey number: **42**

When Robinson donned 42 in 1947, breaking major league baseball's color barrier, it became the most symbolic jersey number in sports. In 1997, MLB retired Robinson's 42 across baseball, and only players who already had the number could continue wearing it, such as New York Yankees closer Mariano Rivera.

2 **Michael Jordan**
NBA guard,
Jersey number: **23**

Number 23 is synonymous with the six-time NBA champion and five-time MVP. But Jordan didn't wear the number throughout his career. In 1990, his jersey was stolen from the Chicago Bulls' locker room, so he had to wear 12 for one game. Jordan also chose 45 after his first comeback from retirement in 1995, before returning to the iconic 23.

3 **Wayne Gretzky**
NHL center,
Jersey number: **99**

As a 16-year-old member of the Sault Ste. Marie Greyhounds in the Ontario Hockey Association, Gretzky wanted to wear 9, the same number as his idol, hockey legend Gordie Howe. However, that number was taken, so his coach suggested adding another 9. The Great One soon made 99 one of the most recognizable jerseys in sports.

4 **Mickey Mantle**
MLB centerfielder,
Jersey number: **7**

Before his major league debut in April 1951, Mantle was given a pinstriped number 6 uniform and tagged as the next Yankees star, following in the footsteps of centerfielder Joe DiMaggio. After three months, a struggling Mantle was sent to the minors. When he returned, he switched his number to 7 and went on to have a Hall of Fame career.

5 **LeBron James**
NBA forward,
Jersey number: **6**

When James joined the Miami Heat in 2010, he gave up the number 23 — which he wore during his seven seasons with the Cleveland Cavaliers — out of respect for Bulls great Michael Jordan. James, however, picked another legendary digit when he chose 6. Hall of Famers Bill Russell and Julius Erving both wore the number.

Y NUMBERS

6 **Babe Ruth**
MLB outfielder,
Jersey number: **3**

The Bambino was numberless until the Yankees decided to revamp their jerseys in 1929 by adding digits. The team issued numbers based on where players regularly hit in the lineup, so Ruth, who hit third, was given number 3. When he retired in 1935, Ruth had hit 714 career homers, a record at the time.

7 **Pelé**
Soccer forward,
Jersey number: **10**

According to Pelé, he received the number 10 jersey — given to a team's playmaker — as a 17-year-old newbie before the 1958 World Cup because it "coincidentally dropped to me." Accident or not, Pelé proved worthy of the number, emerging as a star at the tournament and leading Brazil to a 5–2 win over Sweden in the final.

8 **Peyton Manning**
NFL quarterback,
Jersey number: **18**

When he was drafted by the Indianapolis Colts in 1998, Manning chose number 18 because his brother Cooper wore it in high school. But in 2012, Peyton joined the Denver Broncos, which had retired the number for Frank Tripucka, Denver's first QB. Knowing that Manning wore 18, Tripucka allowed him to have the number.

9 **Mario Lemieux**
NHL center,
Jersey number: **66**

Drawing media attention as a possible challenger to Wayne Gretzky's title as the greatest player in the NHL, Lemieux ditched his number 27 in 1981 to mimic his soon-to-be rival's: Lemieux's agent, who also represented Gretzky, suggested Lemieux take 66, the Great One's number upside down.

10 **Jim Otto**
NFL center,
Jersey number: **00**

In the 1960s and '70s, Otto captivated fans as the anchor of the Oakland Raiders' offensive line. He also drew attention because of his unique number — a zero is also known as both "aught" and "O," the sounds that make up the 12-time Pro Bowler's last name. Double zero is no longer allowed in the NFL.

TOP RI

1 New York Yankees vs. Boston Red Sox
New York led the series 1,145-959-14 through 2012

Foes for more than 100 years, the Yankees and Red Sox have the most heated rivalry in sports. New York, with its 27 World Series titles, may hold the upper hand, but fortunes tipped in Boston's favor when it reversed a 3–0 series deficit against the Yankees in the 2004 American League Championship Series en route to winning its first World Series in 86 years.

10 VALRIES

2 North Carolina vs. Duke
North Carolina led the series 132–104 through 2012–13

These two storied programs are the most bitter rivals in college hoops. The schools, separated by only 10 miles along Tobacco Road, have nine men's basketball national titles between them and have been coached by a combined five Hall of Famers.

3 Boston Celtics vs. Los Angeles Lakers
Boston led the series 198–155 through 2012–13

The Celtics and Lakers franchises are the crown jewels of the NBA. Collectively they have won nearly half of the NBA championships ever awarded. The teams have faced off in the Finals 12 times. Three of those meetings came in the 1980s, fueled by the famous rivalry between the Celtics' Larry Bird and the Lakers' Magic Johnson.

5 Montreal Canadiens vs. Toronto Maple Leafs
Montreal led the series 340–283–88–8 through 2012–13

In Canada, where hockey is the unofficial national pastime, this is the ultimate rivalry. The Leafs and Canadiens are both Original Six teams, hail from the country's biggest cities, and represent two of Canada's heritages — the English and the French. The teams have played each other in six Stanley Cup finals, with Toronto besting Montreal four times. The Canadiens, however, hold the advantage in overall Cup wins — they have the most in league history with 24.

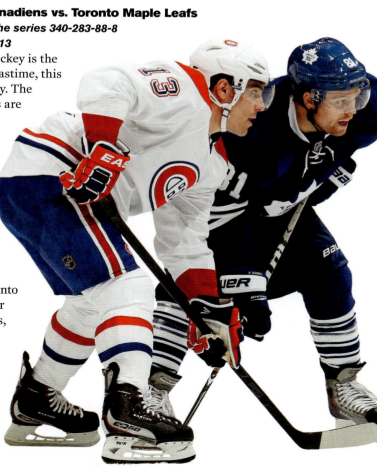

4 Michigan vs. Ohio State
Michigan led the series 58-44-6 through 2012–13

This rivalry is so intense that the annual college football showdown between the two schools is known simply as "The Game." When they clash, Big Ten titles and Rose Bowl berths often hang in the balance. In 2006, a spot in the national championship game was at stake, with Number 1 Ohio State knocking off Number 2 Michigan 42–39.

6 Martina Navratilova vs. Chris Evert
Navratilova won the series 43–37

Navratilova *(far right)* and Evert not only were the marquee women's tennis players for most of the 1970s and '80s, they also were two of the greatest to play the game. They met in 80 matches, including an unprecedented 14 Grand Slam finals between 1975 and '86. With their intense battles, the pair brought international attention to women's tennis and helped the sport grow.

7 **Manchester United vs. Manchester City**
Manchester United led the series 69-46-50 through 2012–13

The deepest sporting rivalry in England — perhaps in all of Europe — exists between United and City. The rivalry dates back to 1881 and has been so contentious that City defender Glyn Pardoe nearly lost a leg after an ugly tackle in a match in 1970. In 2012, the two sides came down to the wire for the Premier League title, with City pulling off a miracle win thanks to two stoppage-time goals.

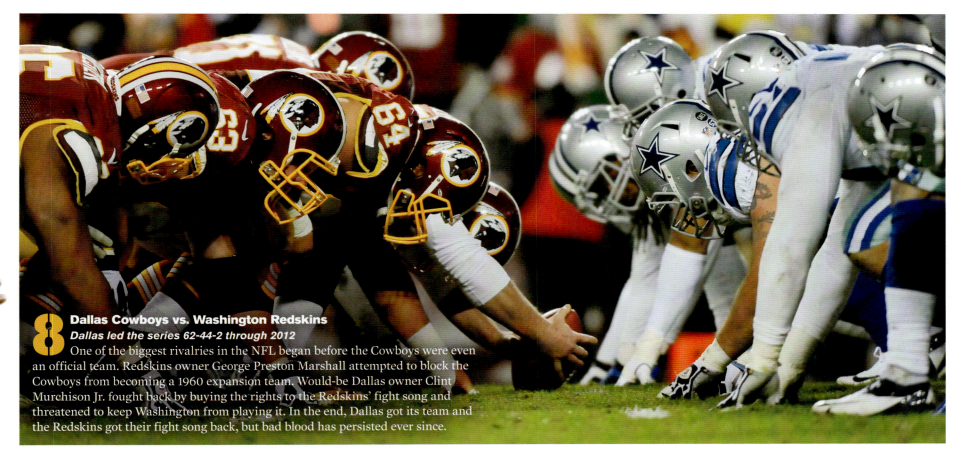

8 Dallas Cowboys vs. Washington Redskins

Dallas led the series 62-44-2 through 2012

One of the biggest rivalries in the NFL began before the Cowboys were even an official team. Redskins owner George Preston Marshall attempted to block the Cowboys from becoming a 1960 expansion team. Would-be Dallas owner Clint Murchison Jr. fought back by buying the rights to the Redskins' fight song and threatened to keep Washington from playing it. In the end, Dallas got its team and the Redskins got their fight song back, but bad blood has persisted ever since.

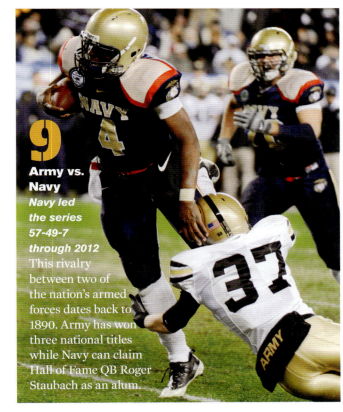

9 Army vs. Navy

Navy led the series 57-49-7 through 2012

This rivalry between two of the nation's armed forces dates back to 1890. Army has won three national titles while Navy can claim Hall of Fame QB Roger Staubach as an alum.

10 San Francisco Giants vs. Los Angeles Dodgers

San Francisco led the series 1,190-1,166-17 through 2012

This rivalry started in the late 1800s when the Dodgers were in Brooklyn and the Giants in Manhattan. Today, these NL West foes clash regularly, with the Giants enjoying more recent success as winners of the World Series in 2010 and 2012.

TOP 10 Mikes

1 Michael Jordan
NBA guard,
Career: 1984–93,
'95–98, 2001–03

In the 1990s, there was a famously catchy song in a Gatorade ad, "Like Mike." It was all about how everyone wanted to be like Mike. And who was Mike? Michael Jordan, the six-time NBA champion, five-time NBA MVP, and the greatest basketball player of all time.

HELLO my name is
Michael Jordan

HELLO my name is
Michael Johnson

HELLO my name is
Michael Phelps

HELLO my name is
Mike Ditka

2 Michael Phelps
Swimmer, Career: 2000–12

Phelps is the most decorated Olympian of all time. But he has plenty of hardware outside of the Games as well. Phelps has won 71 medals in major international long-course competitions (including 57 gold).

3 Michael Johnson
Sprinter, Career: 1989–2000

Johnson is one of the greatest track stars ever. At the 1996 Atlanta Games, he became the only man ever to win the 200 and 400 meters at the same Olympics. He's also the only runner to win the 400 in back-to-back Olympics.

4 Mike Ditka
NFL tight end, Career: 1961–72

Ditka is most famous as the mustachioed, sweater vest–wearing head coach who led the Chicago Bears to Super Bowl XX. But many forget that Iron Mike was a great player as well. He made the Pro Bowl in each of his first five seasons with the Bears and was the first tight end inducted into the Pro Football Hall of Fame.

5 Mike Schmidt
MLB third baseman, Career: 1972–89

A first-ballot Hall of Famer, Schmidt was a power-hitting third baseman for the Philadelphia Phillies and one of the best players of his generation. A three-time National League MVP, he led the league in home runs eight times over his 18-year career.

6 Mike Singletary
NFL linebacker, Career: 1981–92

Singletary was the heart of the Chicago Bears' feared defense during the 1980s. He was considered small for a middle linebacker (6' 0", 230 pounds), but he became famous for his wide-eyed glares and fierce hits. He was twice named NFL Defensive Player of the Year (1985, '88).

7 Mike Piazza
MLB catcher, Career: 1992–2007

There were 1,389 players taken ahead of Piazza, a 62nd-round pick in the 1988 MLB draft. But it was Piazza who would go down as the greatest hitting catcher of all time. He has the most home runs as a backstop (396 of his overall 427) in baseball history.

8 Michael Strahan
NFL defensive end, Career: 1993–2007

These days, Strahan might be better known as a friendly host with a gap-toothed smile on his morning talk show, *Live with Kelly and Michael*. But when he was a defensive end for the New York Giants, quarterbacks never wanted to see him. His 22.5 sacks in 2001 is the single-season record.

9 Mike Bossy
NHL right wing, Career: 1977–87

The New York Islanders won four straight Stanley Cups, from 1979–80 through '82–83, thanks to their Hall of Fame right wing. Bossy became the second player in NHL history to score Cup-clinching goals in back-to-back years ('81–82 and '82–83). He also netted four game-winning goals in one playoff series (the '82–83 Wales Conference finals).

10 Michael Schumacher
Formula One driver, Career: 1991–2006, 2010–12

The fastest Michael? That would be Schumacher, who zoomed into the Formula One record books during his 19-year career. Among the legend's many marks: F1 titles (seven, including five straight from 2000 to '04), career race wins (91), top-three finishes (155), and wins in a season (13).

TOP 10 CELEBRATIONS

1 Gatorade shower

A coach is often the first one to hit the showers when his team wins, thanks to the tradition of players' surprising him on the field with a bucket of ice-cold liquid poured over his head. These days, coaches at all levels get soaked after a big win, as Oklahoma Sooners coach Bob Stoops has experienced *(right)*. However, the tradition is said to have begun with the 1985 New York Giants. The team's head coach, Bill Parcells, had criticized nose tackle Jim Burt before a game against the rival Washington Redskins. After the Giants defeated the Skins, Burt got back at his cranky coach by pouring a cooler full of Gatorade over him. The team won again the following week, and Burt enlisted linebacker Harry Carson as an assistant. The next season, Carson continued to stalk Parcells after wins to drench him. Along the way, the Gatorade dunk became part of sports culture, and even made it all the way to 1600 Pennsylvania Avenue. When the Giants visited the White House after winning the Super Bowl, Carson couldn't resist giving President Ronald Reagan the same treatment. Luckily for the President, Carson showed a little restraint, filling the Gatorade bucket with popcorn instead of liquid.

2 **The Lambeau Leap**
Surprisingly, the famed Green Bay Packers celebration — in which a player jumps into the arms of Packers fans after scoring a touchdown — wasn't started by an offensive player. The first Lambeau Leaper was All-Pro strong safety LeRoy Butler. In 1993, the Packers led the Los Angeles Raiders 14–0 when legendary Green Bay defensive end Reggie White recovered a fumble. White rumbled a few yards before lateraling the ball to Butler, who ran 25 yards for his first career touchdown. Butler was so excited that he leaped into the end zone crowd, which held him up while they cheered. While the NFL has cracked down in recent years on excessive celebration after TDs, the Leap's famous status keeps it from resulting in a 15-yard "unsportsmanlike conduct" penalty, allowing for stars like QB Aaron Rodgers *(right)* to feel the love from Green Bay fans.

3 **Drinking milk at the Indy 500** After driving 500 miles, it's no surprise that winners of the Indianapolis 500, such as three-time champion Dario Franchitti *(above)*, are thirsty. What is unusual is the choice of beverage they drink to celebrate. After taking the checkered flag, Indy 500 winners receive a custom-made bottle of milk with their name printed on the side — and then chug it in victory lane. The tradition began in 1936 when driver Louis Meyer won his third Indianapolis 500 and requested a glass of buttermilk to help him cool down. When an executive at the Milk Foundation saw a picture of Meyer taking a swig, he vowed the winner would drink milk every year. Except for a brief break between 1946 and '56, the tradition has continued ever since.

4 **The Red Wings' octopus toss** Back in the "Original Six" era of the NHL, when there were only six teams in the league, the playoffs consisted of just two seven-game series. To hoist the Stanley Cup, teams had to win eight playoff games. How many tentacles does an octopus have? Eight. So in 1952, two brothers and Red Wings fans figured out a way to pair the two. Pete and Jerry Cusimano owned a fish and poultry market, and when Pete was reminded of the number of wins his Red Wings needed to clinch the title, he thought of the eight octopus tentacles that he saw while stocking seafood. So on April 13, 1952, during Game 3 of the Cup finals, Pete threw an octopus onto the ice after right wing Gordie Howe scored. The fans loved it. When the Red Wings went on to win the game and eventually the Cup, a new tradition was born. Ever since, Detroit fans have brought the eight-legged creatures into Joe Louis Arena to toss onto the ice during home playoff games.

5 Cutting down the nets at the NCAA tournament

Just ask Louisville coach Rick Pitino (below): In college basketball, the only sound sweeter than the swish of the net is the snipping of scissors after winning a title. During college basketball's March Madness, players and coaches scale ladders to cut down the nets and claim a souvenir of a conference title, a Final Four berth, or an NCAA championship. The ritual can be traced back to two hoops hotbeds: North Carolina and Indiana. When North Carolina State won the 1947 Southern Conference crown, the players hoisted their coach, Everett Case, up to the hoop so he could cut down the net. Prior to coming to N.C. State, Case had led Frankfort (Indiana) High School to four state titles between 1925 and '39, and snipping the twine was a tradition in the Hoosier state. When Case was promoted to the college game, he saw no reason to change his ways and, in so doing, gave birth to one of college basketball's most enduring moments.

6 Usain Bolt's point

Usain Bolt's astounding triple-gold-medal performance at the 2008 Beijing Olympics was an iconic moment in track and field history that deserved an equally iconic celebration. Bolt provided one. He extended his left hand with a point and leaned back, while cocking his right hand back as if he were shooting an arrow into the sky. The pose mimicked the path of lightning flashing through the atmosphere — fitting for a man named Bolt, who happens to be the world's fastest man. That pose became his signature, plastered on T-shirts, billboards, and life-sized cardboard cutouts.

7 Spiking the football

The simple gesture of slamming a football down on the ground has become a universal symbol of celebration. The first spike is widely believed to have happened in 1965. New York Giants Pro Bowl wide receiver Homer Jones scored a touchdown and wanted to celebrate, but he knew that the league had banned chucking the ball into the stands. So instead he threw the ball down on the ground and called it a spike. While the NCAA has banned spiking the football, deeming it "excessive celebration," the NFL has allowed the practice to continue, as long as a player doesn't slam the ball down in his opponent's direction. And while touchdown celebrations have become more elaborate, the spike, as demonstrated here by New Orleans Saints running back Darren Sproles, has remained the gold standard.

8 Pie in the face

A common antic among circus clowns, the pie to the face has become a popular form of hijinks in baseball as well. Pitcher A.J. Burnett popularized "pie-ing" in 2009 while playing for the Yankees. Whenever New York had a walk-off win, Burnett would sneak up on the game's hero and splat him with a pie. Nick Swisher (above) was one of his frequent victims. However, getting pied didn't always result in a tasty treat. Burnett often used a towel filled with shaving cream.

9 Carl Edwards's backflip

In 2003, NASCAR driver Carl Edwards was racing in the sport's minor league, the Craftsman Truck Series. That year he got his first win, taking the checkered flag at Kentucky Speedway. Edwards, hardly able to contain his excitement, pulled over short of pit row, climbed out of his truck, stood on the bed, and backflipped off it. Edwards got the idea from fellow driver Tyler Walker, who had made a tradition of backflipping off his car too. Since joining NASCAR's top circuit in 2005, Edwards has continued to flip after each victory.

10 Tearing down the goalpost

College football fans, such as the Kansas State faithful (above), can be so overcome with joy when their team pulls off a huge upset that they often rush the field to celebrate. Sometimes the celebrations get so raucous that it leads to the tearing down of the goalpost. It's not the safest way to mark the occasion — goalposts can weigh between 450 and 1,800 pounds — but if the fans do get them down safely, some crazy things can happen. When Georgia Tech beat Virginia Tech at its 2009 homecoming game, students carried the goalposts to the university president's house and dropped them off in his front yard.

TOP 10 NICKNAMES

Refrigerator

1. William Perry
NFL defensive lineman,
Career: 1985–94

One day during his freshman year at Clemson, the 6'2", 335-pound Perry was sharing an elevator with teammate Ray Brown. Barely able to fit in next to Perry, Brown told the defensive lineman that he was as big as a refrigerator, and a nickname was born. After Perry won the 1985 Super Bowl with the Chicago Bears, he was fitted with a size-25 championship ring — more than double the average man's ring size.

Babe

2. George Herman Ruth
MLB outfielder,
Career: 1914–35

Ruth's nickname is so famous that everyone — even decades later — knows him by that singular name: Babe. As a 19-year-old phenom, he signed a $600 contract to pitch for Jack Dunn's minor league Baltimore Orioles club. A Baltimore sportswriter dubbed him one of Dunn's "babes." Ruth grew into one of the greatest sluggers of all time, hitting 714 home runs in his career, a record that stood for 39 years.

Wizard of Oz

3. Ozzie Smith
MLB shortstop,
Career: 1978–96

Smith revolutionized the shortstop position and hexed opponents with his stellar defense. He won 13 consecutive Gold Gloves and retired in 1996 with six career fielding records for shortstops, including most assists (8,375) and double plays (1,590). A fan favorite, he was also famous for making acrobatic entrances, drawing cheers as he did backflips after running onto the field.

THE GREAT ONE

4 Wayne Gretzky
NHL center,
Career: 1978–99

Canadian newspapers were already calling Wayne "The Great Gretzky" at the age of 11. He later became known as the Great One, and he more than lived up to the elegantly simple nickname. Perhaps the most talented player ever to put on hockey skates, Gretzky owns or shares 60 NHL records, led the league in scoring 10 times, and won four Stanley Cups.

ATOMIC FLEA

5 Lionel Messi
Soccer forward,
Career: 2003–present

The 5'7" Messi got his nickname, *Pulga Atomica*, which means "atomic flea" in Spanish, because of his size, speed, and pesky ability to score goals. The quick forward for FC Barcelona and Argentina has not let his small stature hold him back from dominating the soccer field. In 2012, he dizzied defenses on his way to netting 91 goals, breaking a four-decade-old scoring record.

Magic

6 Earvin Johnson
NBA guard,
Career: 1979–96

A sportswriter assigned the nickname Magic to Johnson after an impressive triple-double performance (36 points, 16 rebounds, and 16 assists) as a 15-year-old high school star. The Hall of Fame point guard's play remained nothing short of magical through college and the pros. He led Michigan State to an NCAA title in 1979, and won five NBA championships with the Los Angeles Lakers.

7 Adrian Peterson
NFL running back,
Career: 2007–present

All Day

Peterson was 2 years old when his parents realized there was no stopping him. "I ran around all the time," Peterson has said about his childhood. Peterson's dad gave his active son the nickname All Day. The All-Pro running back has never slowed down. Not even ACL and MCL tears to his left knee in 2011 could hold him back. He returned in 2012 and fell just nine yards shy of breaking the NFL single-season rushing record.

Flying Tomato

8 Shaun White
Snowboarder and skateboarder,
Career: 2003–present

With a shock of red hair trailing him as he soared through the air, White became known as the Flying Tomato. Even though he cut his long locks in 2012 and has never fully embraced the nickname, the catchy moniker continues to stick with the two-time Winter Olympics gold medalist and 24-time X Games medalist.

THE TRUTH

9 Paul Pierce
NBA forward,
Career: 1998–present

Pierce doesn't have to lie about his game. Just ask former NBA center Shaquille O'Neal. During his third year in the league, Pierce unleashed a 42-point performance on 13-for-19 shooting against O'Neal's Los Angeles Lakers, inspiring the center to label him the Truth.

Six Feet of Sunshine

10 Kerri Walsh-Jennings
Olympic beach volleyball player,
Career: 2000–present

Walsh-Jennings and Misty May-Treanor make up the greatest beach volleyball team of all time. Even though she is fierce in the sand, the 6'3" Walsh-Jennings is all smiles off it — which is why her husband, volleyball player Casey Jennings, calls her Six Feet of Sunshine.

1 Gordie Howe
NHL right wing, Career: 1946–80, '97

The longtime Detroit Red Wings great was an offensive threat for more than four decades. He scored his first NHL goal when he was 18 years old, and his last one — his 801st — when he was 51. Mr. Hockey won six scoring titles and a half-dozen MVP trophies, and led Detroit to four Stanley Cup championships. In 1973, at the age of 45, Howe left the NHL and played six seasons in the World Hockey Association. He earned MVP honors in his first year, and in 1975–76 he had a 102-point season. Howe played for so long that he got to suit up alongside his sons, Mark and Marty, for seven seasons. Howe reached another milestone in 1997 at age 69, when he played pro hockey in a sixth decade after signing with the IHL's Detroit Vipers and returning to the ice for one shift.

4 Nolan Ryan
MLB pitcher, Career: 1966–93

Ryan racked up a record 5,714 strikeouts in his career, and 1,437 of them came after the age of 40. When he was 40 years old and pitching for the Houston Astros in 1987, Ryan led the National League in ERA (2.76) and strikeouts (270). Two years later, as a member of the Texas Rangers, he threw 301 strikeouts (one of only 33 300-strikeout seasons in the modern era). His career spanned 27 seasons and four decades, until he retired at age 46.

TOP 10 OLD

2 Satchel Paige
Negro Leagues and MLB pitcher,
Career: 1926–53, '65

The fireballing righty dominated the Negro Leagues in the 1930s and '40s, but didn't make his MLB debut until 1948, as a 42-year-old. After pitching for the Cleveland Indians, he joined the St. Louis Browns and went to back-to-back All-Star Games in 1952 and '53, when he was 46 and 47. He retired but returned for one game for the Kansas City Athletics in 1965, when he was 59. Athletics owner Charlie Finley gave him a rocking chair to use in the bullpen before Paige went out and pitched three shutout innings.

3 George Blanda,
NFL quarterback and kicker,
Career: 1949–75

The Hall of Famer played a remarkable 26 seasons in the AFL and NFL. Blanda joined the Oakland Raiders in 1967 and turned 40 that September. He went on to kick for them until he was 48 years old, and in 1970 he also became the oldest quarterback in conference-title-game history. After starter Daryle Lamonica got hurt, the 43-year-old Blanda entered the game and threw for 271 yards and two touchdowns.

5 Julio Franco
MLB infielder,
Career: 1982–2007

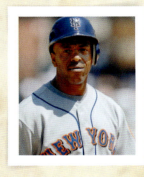

One reason Franco had more than 4,000 hits between the majors, minors, Mexico, Japan, the Dominican Republic, and South Korea was because he played until he was almost 50. Franco is thought to be the oldest position player in major league history, playing his last season in 2007 with the Atlanta Braves at age 48.

6 Dara Torres
Swimmer,
Career: 1984–2012

When it comes to swimming, 30-year-olds are considered over the hill, so it was impressive when Torres, at age 33, won five medals at the 2000 Sydney Games, more than any other member of the U.S. team. But even more remarkable was her winning two silvers at the Beijing Games eight years later. At age 41, Torres was the first female swimmer over the age of 40 to compete in the Olympics.

7 George Foreman
Boxer,
Career: 1969–77, '87–97

Foreman won his first heavyweight belt as a 22-year-old in 1971, and won another title belt in 1997, when he was 48. In his final bout, in November 1997, he lost to Shannon Briggs in a majority decision, even though many felt that Foreman actually won that fight. It was his only loss after the age of 45.

8 Nancy Lieberman
WNBA point guard, Career: 1975–97

Lieberman was a women's basketball all-time great during the 1970s and '80s, starring for the U.S. Olympic team and in pro leagues, both men's and women's. When the WNBA formed in 1997, she joined the league at age 39. She retired after the first season, but came back 11 years later at age 50, playing one game for the Detroit Shock.

9 Jamie Moyer
MLB pitcher, Career: 1986–2012

It was a surprise when the 49-year-old Moyer made the Colorado Rockies rotation out of spring training in 2012. After all, Moyer had made his big-league debut in 1986, before seven of his Colorado teammates were even born. On May 16, 2012, he made MLB history. Moyer not only became the oldest player to record a win (the Rockies beat the Arizona Diamondbacks 6–1), but he also became the oldest player to drive in a run when he hit a two-run single.

FOLKS

10 Ed Whitlock
Marathoner,
Career: 1972–present

This long-distance runner didn't take the sport seriously until he was in his 40s, but now the octogenarian can't be stopped. Whitlock owns master's-level records for fastest marathon times for the 70-to-74, 75-to-79, and 80-to-84 age groups. At age 69, he became the oldest person to run a marathon in less than three hours.

LeBron James
NBA forward

Declared THE CHOSEN ONE on the cover of SPORTS ILLUSTRATED as a 17-year-old, James was a legend in the making. As a freshman at St. Vincent–St. Mary High in Akron, Ohio, he averaged 18.0 points and 6.2 rebounds per game, leading his team to an undefeated record and a state championship. By the time he was a senior, James was an all-around star with 31.6 points, 9.6 rebounds, 4.6 assists, and 3.4 steals a game. After being selected straight out of high school by the Cleveland Cavaliers as the Number 1 pick in the 2003 NBA draft, the 19-year-old went on to become the youngest player in the league to earn the Rookie of the Year Award.

Top 10 Prodigies

2 Tiger Woods
Golfer

Woods's career began at the age of 2, when he appeared on a TV show competing against Bob Hope in a putting contest. By 9, Woods had won the Junior World Golf Championships, and six years later he took home the U.S. Amateur trophy. Woods soon became the youngest player ever to win the Masters, launching him to the top of golf's world ranking at age 20 — the fastest ascent to Number 1 in the sport.

3 Wayne Gretzky
NHL center

It didn't take long for Gretzky to become the Great One. When he was 11, Gretzky netted 378 goals in his peewee league in Brantford, Ontario, Canada, including one game in which he scored three goals in 45 seconds. Six years later, the 17-year-old phenom became the youngest player on Team Canada at the 1978 World Junior Championships. He led all scorers with eight goals and nine assists in six games. When Gretzky retired from the NHL in 1999, he held 40 regular-season records.

4 Venus and Serena Williams
Tennis players

Venus and Serena were 12 and 10 years old, respectively, when they each won their singles division in the Southern Junior Sectional Championships. With a serve that topped 100 miles per hour, Venus turned pro at age 14. In 1997, the 17-year-old became the first unseeded women's tennis player in 40 years to reach the U.S. Open final. Little sister Serena was not far behind. At age 18, she won the 1999 U.S. Open. The sisters have 22 Grand Slam singles titles total and have faced each other in eight of those finals, with Serena besting Venus six times.

5 Sidney Crosby
NHL center

When the Pittsburgh Penguins drafted the 17-year-old in 2005, he was known as the Next One. That's because the phenom scored 120 goals in 121 games in the Quebec Major Junior Hockey League, showing the potential to have a career as stellar as the Great One. In 2009, Crosby became the youngest captain in NHL history to lead his team to a Stanley Cup title.

6 Kobe Bryant
NBA guard

Bryant played in packed high school gyms as a guard for Lower Merion (Pennsylvania) High, wowing crowds with his one-handed jams and no-look passes. He proved to be not only an entertainer but also a winner, leading his team to its first state title in 53 years. The hoops star was just getting started. Bryant went straight to the pros in 1996, and has become a five-time NBA champion and two-time scoring champion.

7 Shaun White
Snowboarder and Skateboarder

White had two open-heart surgeries before his first birthday, but that never slowed him down. He scored his first sponsorship at age 7, and burst onto the snowboarding scene as a pro at 13. White took home Olympic gold in the halfpipe as a 19-year-old in 2006 and repeated in 2010. He also became the face of skateboarding. At age 18, he won silver in vert at the 2005 Summer X Games, and two years later took home gold.

8 Missy Franklin
Swimmer

Franklin was 5 when her mother, who was afraid of water, signed her up for swim classes. Since then, Franklin has made a major splash in the pool. She qualified for the 2012 Olympic team by breaking the U.S. record in the 100-meter backstroke at age 17. At the London Games, she set world records in the 400-meter medley relay and 200-meter backstroke. She took home four gold medals and one bronze.

9 Ryan Sheckler
Skateboarder

As a toddler, Sheckler was rolling on a skateboard in his parents' driveway. At 4 he was doing ollies, and by 7 he was skateboarding on a mini-ramp in his backyard every day. A pro at 13, Sheckler has won six Summer X Games medals and is the youngest gold medalist in the history of the competition.

10 Bryce Harper
MLB leftfielder

Harper has always played with the big boys. At age 3, he faced 6-year-olds in tee-ball. During one tournament in Alabama, a 12-year-old Harper went 12-for-12, including 11 home runs (yes, 11) that soared more than 250 feet. He also torched the base paths. At Las Vegas (Nevada) High, Harper scored on six wild pitches from second base in one season. After about two years in the minors, the Washington Nationals leftfielder finished his first big-league season as the 2012 National League Rookie of the Year.

1 **Joe DiMaggio's 56-game hit streak**

Joltin' Joe owns one of the greatest — and most difficult to break — records in sports. From May 15 to July 16, 1941, the New York Yankees centerfielder hit safely in 56 consecutive games. But he didn't merely reach base. Over that span, DiMaggio hit .408 with 15 home runs (including the one pictured here) and 55 RBIs. The closest anyone has come to DiMaggio's mark was a 44-game hit streak by the Cincinnati Reds' Pete Rose in 1978.

Top10 Records

2 **Wayne Gretzky's 215 points in a season**

In the 1985–86 season, Gretzky set single-season records for points (215) and assists (163). Before the Great One came along, Boston Bruins center Phil Esposito owned the single-season points record with 152 in 1970–71. Gretzky broke that mark in 1980–81 with 164 points and went on to top that number seven more times.

3 **Cal Ripken's 2,632 consecutive games played**

Ripken played in every single game for the Baltimore Orioles for more than 17 years before finally choosing to end his streak late in the 1998 season. An MLB fan voting contest named September 6, 1995, the night he broke Lou Gehrig's mark, as the most memorable moment in baseball history.

4 **UConn women's basketball team's 90-game win streak**

The Huskies' stretch started on November 16, 2008, with an 82–71 win over Georgia Tech and ended on December 30, 2010, with a 71–59 loss to Stanford. It included two NCAA titles and more than two years as the nation's top-ranked team.

5 **Wilt Chamberlain's 100-point game**

The famous scoring effort came on March 2, 1962, in a 169–147 win for the Philadelphia Warriors over the New York Knicks. Chamberlain hit his 100th point in style — an alley-oop with 30 seconds left to play. That season he set an NBA mark with 50.4 points per game.

6 **Nolan Ryan's 5,714 career strikeouts**

With a career that spanned 27 years, Ryan rung up more strikeouts than any other pitcher in baseball history. He led the league in strikeouts 11 times. Ryan's nearly unhittable pitches also helped him throw a record seven no-hitters during his career.

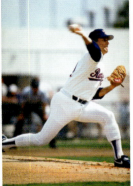

7 **Roger Federer's 17 Grand Slam singles titles**

Federer is considered to be the greatest tennis player of all time, with 17 Grand Slam singles titles through 2012. The Swiss player's dominance has been especially noticeable at Wimbledon and the U.S. Open, both of which he won five consecutive times.

8 **Cy Young's 511 wins**

Thanks in part to the era he pitched in (1890 to 1911), when a starter could easily appear in 50 games, Young's 511 career victories are unlikely to be matched again. The righthander won more than 30 games in five different seasons, including his 36–12 campaign in 1892.

9 **Kelly Slater's 11 world champion surfing titles**

Slater is the youngest (age 20) and the oldest (age 39) surfer to win ASP World Championships. In between he also won five consecutive titles from 1994 through '98. His 11 championships are more than double any other male surfer in the history of the sport.

10 **Bob Gibson's 1.12 ERA**

Gibson allowed only 38 earned runs in 304⅔ innings of work in 1968, the lowest for any pitcher since the dead-ball era. Over the course of the season, Gibson became one of the most feared hurlers in baseball. He had 13 shutouts and struck out 268 batters, using just two pitches: a fastball and a slider.

TOP 10 JOURN

1

Octavio Dotel
MLB pitcher,
Career: 1999–present

In the late 1990s, the flame throwing righty was the star of the New York Mets' farm system. After appearing for the Mets during the 1999 season, he became the prize in a blockbuster trade to the Houston Astros. Dotel would go on to be traded five more times, and when he signed with the Detroit Tigers before the 2012 season, he set an MLB record by joining his 13th franchise.

2

Mike Sillinger
NHL center,
Career: 1990–2009

Sillinger is sometimes referred to as Suitcase Sillinger. It's not difficult to see why. The center spent 17 years in the NHL, and in only nine of those seasons did he start and finish the season playing for the same team. Sillinger was traded a record 10 times, and eventually suited up for 12 NHL franchises.

3

Peter Shilton
Soccer goalie,
Career: 1966–97

With a successful — and long — career, Shilton is one of the most famous goalkeepers in the history of soccer. Along with appearing in a record 125 matches for England's national team, he played for 11 club teams during his 30-year career, ultimately appearing in 1,005 matches and retiring at age 47.

4

Matt Millen
NFL linebacker,
Career: 1980–91

Millen won Super Bowls with the Oakland Raiders (twice), San Francisco 49ers, and Washington Redskins, making him the only player to win NFL titles with three different teams. Millen wasn't just along for the ride. The two-time All-Pro was one of the NFL's best inside linebackers in the 1980s and early '90s.

5

Jose Bautista
MLB outfielder,
Career: 2004–present

MLB teams didn't think much of Bautista at the start of his career. In 2004 alone, he played for four franchises. Then in 2010, his second full season in Toronto, he made an adjustment to his swing that resulted in an MLB-leading 54 homers, nearly 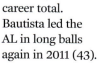 doubling his career total. Bautista led the AL in long balls again in 2011 (43).

EYMEN

6 J.T. O'Sullivan
*NFL quarterback,
Career: 2002–12*

You may never have heard of the longtime backup quarterback, but there's a good chance he played on your favorite football team. Although he made only eight career starts (all with the San Francisco 49ers in 2008), O'Sullivan was on a record 11 teams during his 10-year NFL career.

7 Tony Massenburg
*NBA forward,
Career: 1990–2005*

Second-round picks don't always stick around the NBA for long. That wasn't the case for the bruising big man who played for 12 different teams (tying an NBA record) during 13 seasons in the league. Massenburg started his NBA journey with the San Antonio Spurs, and finished there too, winning an NBA title in 2004–05.

8 Robert Horry
*NBA forward,
Career: 1992–2008*

Horry is tied for seventh all-time with seven NBA championships, which he won with three teams (the Houston Rockets, Los Angeles Lakers, and San Antonio Spurs). Horry earned the nickname Big Shot Bob in honor of the many clutch shots he hit during his teams' NBA championship runs.

9 Joe Smith
*NBA forward,
Career: 1995–2011*

When the Golden State Warriors drafted Smith with the top pick in 1995, they hoped he would earn a spot in the record books. But they probably didn't expect this mark: Smith played for 12 franchises, tying an NBA record. He did two stints each with the Minnesota Timberwolves, Philadelphia 76ers, and Cleveland Cavaliers.

10 Joel Youngblood
*MLB outfielder,
Career: 1976–89*

Youngblood played for six teams during his 14-year career, which included one notable feat. On August 4, 1982, he got a hit for the New York Mets in a day game. During the game he was traded to the Montreal Expos. He joined them that night and got another hit. He is the only player to have hits for two teams in two cities on the same day.

2 Olympic gold medal

Olympic gold is the most coveted prize for athletes, from archers to wrestlers. A winner at the ancient Olympics received a wreath, but medals were awarded when the modern Games began in 1896. Today, the winner's medal has to have at least six grams of gold. For the Summer Games, one side of the medal must depict Nike, the winged Greek goddess of victory. The Winter Olympics medals have no design rules, so they've come in all shapes and sizes.

3 World Series trophy

Officially called the Commissioner's Trophy, the hardware presented to Major League Baseball's World Series champion features 30 flags that represent each team. The 30-pound award is 24 inches tall and 11 inches in diameter. MLB debuted the current design of the trophy in 1999.

1 Stanley Cup

The original Stanley Cup, donated by Lord Stanley of Preston, was a bowl on top of a trophy. It has since become the most iconic trophy in sports. First presented in 1893, the Cup has expanded over the years to accommodate the names of each member of the winning team. Today it weighs 34¼ pounds and stands 35½ inches in height. When room needs to be made for engraving the names of the newest winners, the oldest band is removed. Perhaps the coolest tradition: Each member of the championship team gets to take the Cup home for 24 hours to share with his friends and family.

4 **Heisman Trophy** Awarded each year to the nation's top college football player, the Heisman Trophy is the most recognizable individual award in U.S. sports. The sculpture was modeled after Ed Smith, a star on the 1934 New York University football team, and named after legendary football coach John W. Heisman.

5 **Lombardi Trophy** The NFL's championship trophy was first conceived during a 1967 lunch meeting between then NFL commissioner Pete Rozelle and Oscar Riedner, vice president of Tiffany and Co., who sketched the design on a napkin. Each year, the jewelry company handcrafts a 22-inch-tall, seven-pound trophy from sterling silver. (It also makes a backup in case one gets damaged.) In 1970, the NFL renamed the award the Vince Lombardi Trophy in honor of the legendary Green Bay Packers coach.

6 **BCS Championship** The gem given to the winner of the BCS Championship Game is an eight-pound Waterford crystal football. Crafted in Europe and worth $30,000, the sculpture has to be handled with care. In 2012, a parent of an Alabama player bumped into the trophy and shattered the crystal.

7 **Claret Jug** When the British Open began, in 1860, winners won a leather belt with a big silver buckle. After Tom Morris won the belt for three straight years a decade later, he got to keep it, forcing the Open to look for another prize. In 1873, they started awarding the Golf Champion Trophy, now known as the Claret Jug.

8 **WBC title belt** Each World Boxing Council weight class title holder receives a championship belt that features the flags of the 161 member

countries of the Council. Any champion who holds the belt for five years or has 12 successful title defenses is given a belt he can keep.

9 **NBA trophy** From 1948 to '77, the NBA awarded a modest bowl on a pedestal to its champions. The league replaced that trophy in 1977 with a sterling-silver model that has a regulation-sized basketball hanging on the rim. In 1984, the NBA named it the Larry O'Brien Trophy in honor of a former commissioner.

10 **Masters green jacket** Worn by members of the Augusta National Golf Club since 1949, the green jacket was first awarded to the Masters champion that same year. The winner is allowed to keep the blazer for one year, then must return it to Augusta the following April.

Top 10 Trophies

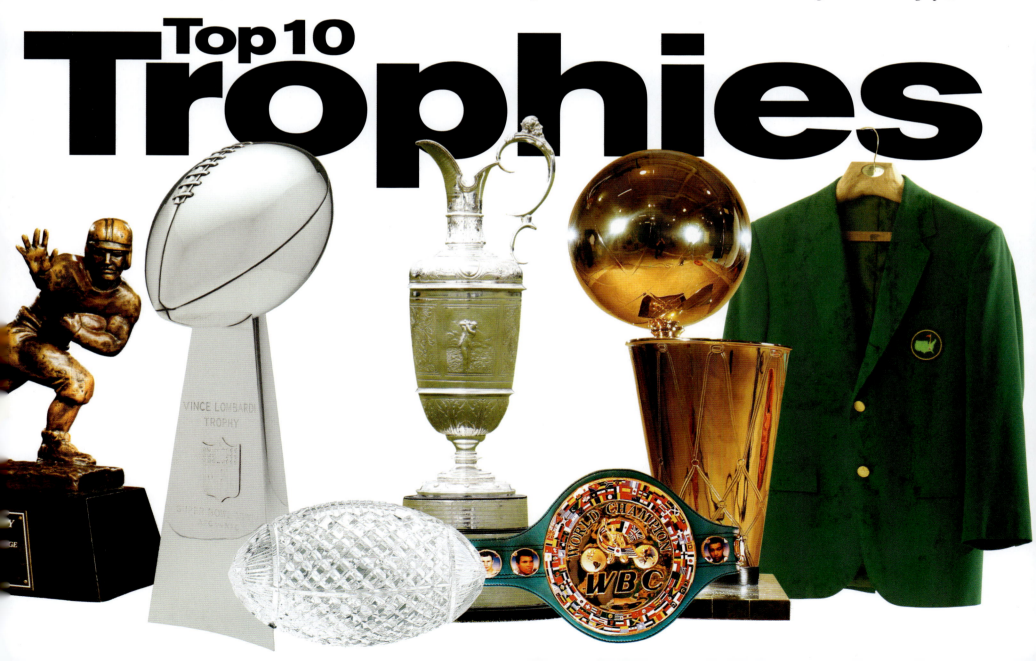

TOP 10
FANS

Oakland Raiders

Don't mess with the Raiders' faithful — the scariest group in football. Clad in spiked armor and face paint, they frighten opponents from the south end zone of O.co Coliseum, known as the Black Hole.

2 Alabama Crimson Tide
"Roll Tide" may be the most common greeting in Alabama, a salute to the state's beloved University of Alabama Crimson Tide teams, especially football. Fans pack Bryant–Denny stadium, which seats 101,821 people, to cheer on the three-time BCS national champions.

3 Pittsburgh Steelers
The Steelers are famous for their widespread fan base that stretches far beyond their Western Pennsylvania home. Pittsburgh fans do their best to take home-field advantage away from their opponents, traveling across the country to rival NFL stadiums to wave their Terrible Towels.

5 Seattle Seahawks
CenturyLink Field, home of the Seahawks, is the loudest building in the NFL, thanks in part to a roof that bounces the sound from the crowd back to the field. In a 2005 game, the visiting New York Giants had 11 false-start penalties because of the raucous crowd.

6 Oklahoma City Thunder
Oklahoma City didn't get an NBA team until 2008, but it already has one of the rowdiest fan bases in the league. In a 2010 playoff game, the noise in the Thunder's home arena was measured at 109 decibels, which is about as loud as a jackhammer.

7 Montreal Canadiens
With 24 Stanley Cup titles, the Canadiens have bred some of the most passionate — and demanding — fans in sports. When 20,000 Canadiens fans fill the Bell Centre with their chants of "Olé," it's an electric atmosphere.

4 Boston Red Sox

Long-suffering Red Sox Nation rejoiced when Boston finally broke the Curse of the Bambino in 2004, winning its first World Series in 86 years. More than a million fans came out to celebrate at the parade that fall. Through the 2012 season, the Red Sox had a record 820-game sellout streak.

8 Liverpool FC

Known for singing Rodgers and Hammerstein's "You'll Never Walk Alone" prior to each match while holding their Liverpool scarves aloft, Liverpool fans have cheered on the Reds to 18 Premier League titles and five European Cups.

9 Michigan Wolverines

The maize-and-blue maniacs who fill the 109,901-seat Big House are some of the most dedicated in college football. But they aren't just gridiron fans. The 2,600-seat Maize Rage section at basketball games gives the Wolverines a big home-court advantage too.

10 St. Louis Cardinals

The Cardinals were the southern- and western-most team in baseball until 1952. As a result, St. Louis fans are from all over the country. Today, loyal Cards fans are so widespread that their games are broadcast on local television and radio in 10 states.

Multi-Sport Athletes

1 Bo Jackson
MLB outfielder and NFL running back; Career: 1982–94

Bo knew how to dominate, whether it was as an outfielder or as a running back. After a Heisman Trophy–winning college career at Auburn, Jackson was selected by the Tampa Bay Buccaneers with the Number 1 pick of the 1986 NFL draft. That same year, the Kansas City Royals took him in the fourth round of the MLB draft. Jackson did not sign with the Bucs and played only baseball in '86. But the following year he signed with the Los Angeles Raiders. In 1987, after hitting 22 home runs with the Royals, Jackson joined the Raiders seven games into the season and rushed for 554 yards. Jackson was so talented that he could step right off the diamond and onto the gridiron without needing training camp or preseason games. He juggled both sports for nearly five years, earning trips to both the All-Star Game (he was MVP in 1989) and the Pro Bowl along the way. A hip injury cut his sports career short, but it did nothing to diminish his accomplishments in football and baseball.

2 Jim Thorpe
Track and field star, MLB outfielder, and NFL halfback; Career: 1912–28

Thorpe's greatest athletic achievements were his gold medals in decathlon and pentathlon at the 1912 Olympics, but he was also golden on the football and baseball fields. Beginning in 1913, Thorpe spent six seasons as an outfielder in the majors, primarily with the New York Giants. He was also a Hall of Fame NFL halfback. Even after becoming the league's first president in 1920, Thorpe continued to play until the 1928 season before retiring at age 41.

TRACK AND FIELD

FOOTBALL

BASEBALL

3 **Babe Didrikson Zaharias**
Track and field star and golfer; Career: 1930–55

You name the sport, and Didrikson Zaharias probably excelled at. She was an All-America basketball player who led her team to the 1931 AAU championship. In 1932 she won Olympic gold medals in the 80-meter hurdles and the javelin. Didrikson Zaharias also stood out in softball, baseball, billiards, tennis, diving, and bowling. But she was best known for her achievements in golf. In a 20-year career, she won 82 golf tournaments, including a streak of 14 in a row.

TRACK AND FIELD

GOLF

4 **Jim Brown**
Lacrosse midfielder and NFL fullback; Career: 1954–65

One of the greatest fullbacks of all time, Brown led the league in rushing eight times and was a three-time NFL MVP. Before becoming a star for the Cleveland Browns, Brown also dominated the lacrosse field at Syracuse University. As a senior he scored 43 goals in 10 games and was named to the All-America team. Brown is a member of both the Pro Football and Lacrosse Halls of Fame.

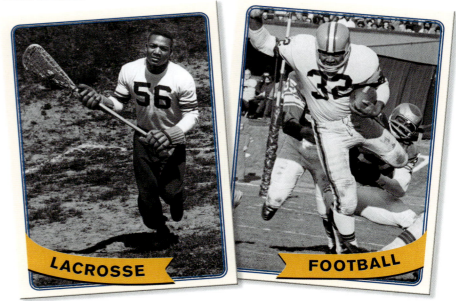

LACROSSE

FOOTBALL

7 **Tony Gonzalez**
College basketball forward and NFL tight end; Career: 1995–present

Gonzalez is a 13-time NFL Pro Bowler and the league record holder for receiving touchdowns by a tight end (103). His trademark TD celebration is dunking the ball over the upright, which is a nod to his hoops days at Cal. As a freshman during the 1995–96 season, Gonzalez shot 64 percent from the floor. Two seasons later, he helped the Golden Bears reach the Sweet 16 of the NCAA tournament.

BASKETBALL

FOOTBALL

8 **Charlie Ward**
College football quarterback and NBA guard; Career: 1989–2005

Before he put on an NBA jersey, Ward quarterbacked Florida State to its first national championship and won the Heisman Trophy. Ward, who also played basketball for the Seminoles, chose to pursue a career in hoops after being drafted in the first round by the New York Knicks. He spent 11 seasons as a reliable NBA point guard. In 2006, he was inducted into the College Football Hall of Fame.

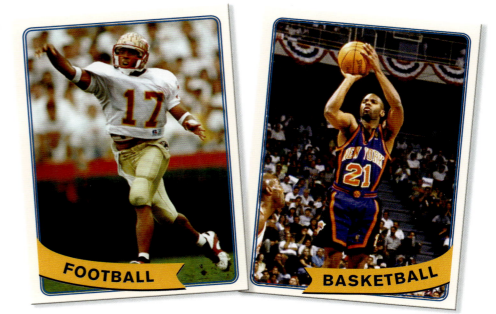

FOOTBALL

BASKETBALL

5 Deion Sanders
NFL cornerback and MLB outfielder; Career: 1989–2005

Primetime is the only athlete to win a Super Bowl and a World Series, and the only player in professional sports to hit a home run and score a touchdown in the same week. Sanders was hard to catch. As a centerfielder, he finished second in the National League in stolen bases twice (1994 and '97). On the football field, his speed helped him reach eight Pro Bowls and win two Super Bowls.

FOOTBALL

BASEBALL

6 Jackie Robinson
College track and field star and MLB second baseman; Career: 1939–56

Before the Brooklyn Dodgers star famously broke major league baseball's color barrier in 1947, he was the first UCLA athlete to earn varsity letters in four sports: baseball, basketball, football, and track. In 1940, Robinson won the long-jump competition at the NCAA men's track and field championship. Seven years later he became the first Rookie of the Year in MLB history.

TRACK AND FIELD

BASEBALL

9 Clara Hughes
Olympic speed skater and cyclist; Career: 1989–present

Hughes is a star for all seasons. Competing for her native Canada in cycling during the summer and speed skating in the winter, she is a five-time Olympian. Hughes took home a gold medal in the 5,000-meter speed skating event at the 2006 Winter Olympics and won two bronzes at the 1996 Summer Games in cycling.

SPEED SKATING

CYCLING

10 Robert Griffin III
College track and field star and NFL quarterback; Career: 2008–present

A big part of why RGIII was able to lead the Washington Redskins to the playoffs as a rookie in 2012 was his speed. The Heisman Trophy winner developed his wheels on the track. As a freshman at Baylor, he won the Big 12 gold medal in the 400-meter hurdles and placed third at the NCAA Outdoor Championships in the event.

TRACK AND FIELD

FOOTBALL

1 1982–83 North Carolina State Wolfpack

Men's college basketball tournament

Facing the mighty University of Houston in the 1983 NCAA men's basketball final, sixth-seeded N.C. State pulled off one of the greatest upsets in tournament history. With the game tied in the final seconds, Wolfpack guard Dereck Whittenburg heaved a long prayer that missed everything. Teammate Lorenzo Charles grabbed the airball and slammed it home just before the buzzer sounded. N.C. State coach Jim Valvano famously ran onto the court, looking for someone to hug to celebrate the 54–52 win.

Top 10 Underdogs

2 Jeremy Lin
NBA guard

In the winter of 2011, the entire country had a case of Linsanity thanks to an undrafted Asian-American point guard from Harvard. After being waived by the Golden State Warriors and the Houston Rockets, Lin was given a chance to start on the injury-plagued New York Knicks. He soon became a global sensation. Lin led the Knicks on a seven-game win streak, scored in double digits in 11 straight games, and hit a game-winning three-point shot against the Toronto Raptors. With each game, his stardom grew, and his name launched a thousand puns (Linsanity, Linning Streak, Jeremy is BallLin'). Fans from New York to China embraced Lin's story of defying the odds and cheered him on as he helped push New York into the playoffs.

3 1980 U.S. Men's Hockey Team
Lake Placid Olympics

At the 1980 Winter Games, the U.S. team of amateurs stunned the Soviet Union, winners of four straight gold medals. A decisive goal by Mike Eruzione capped the "Miracle on Ice," giving the Americans a 4–3 victory in the semifinals. The U.S. then beat Sweden to win gold.

4 1968 New York Jets
Super Bowl III

New York Jets quarterback Joe Namath raised the stakes when he famously guaranteed that his team would defeat the heavily favored Baltimore Colts, who had finished the regular season 15–1, in the Super Bowl. Broadway Joe stuck to his promise. Beating the Colts' blitz and passing for 206 yards, he led the Jets to a 16–7 upset win. Namath was named Super Bowl MVP as the Jets captured the first championship title for the AFL.

5 Buster Douglas
Boxer

No one thought Douglas had a chance against undefeated and undisputed heavyweight champion Mike Tyson in 1990. But during the bout, Douglas delivered an uppercut followed by three straight shots to Tyson for the knockout in the 10th round to pull off the upset and win the heavyweight title.

6 Kurt Warner
NFL quarterback

Undrafted in 1994, Warner took a job stocking shelves at an Iowa grocery store, but he never let go of his NFL dreams. After four years in the Arena Football League, the St. Louis Rams gave him a shot in 1998. In six seasons, Warner was a two-time NFL MVP and played in three Super Bowls, winning one.

7 Gabrielle Douglas
Olympic gymnast

The 16-year-old Douglas quietly rose to stardom at the 2012 Olympics. First, she helped lead the U.S. to its first team gold since 1996. Then, two nights later, she gave nearly flawless performances on her way to earning another gold in the all-around competition, becoming the first African American to win the event.

8 1984–85 Villanova Wildcats
Men's college basketball tournament

The game was played on April Fool's Day, but eighth-seeded Villanova's upset win over Number 1 Georgetown in the 1985 NCAA title game was no joke. The Wildcats, led by center Ed Pinckney (54), shot 79 percent from the field to beat center Patrick Ewing (33) and the Hoyas 66–64.

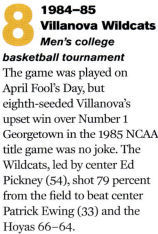

9 1997–98 Harvard Crimson
Women's college basketball tournament

In the history of the men's and women's NCAA tournaments, only once has a 16 seed knocked out a Number 1. That distinction belongs to the 1998 Harvard women's team. When the Crimson traveled to Stanford, no team from the Ivy League had ever won a tournament game. With just under four minutes to go, Harvard went on a 9–2 run to win 71–67.

10 Rulon Gardner
Olympic wrestler

Gardner grew up on a dairy farm in Wyoming, where he wrestled 2,000-pound cows for fun. The training came in handy at the 2000 Olympics, when he wrestled three-time gold medalist Alexander Karelin. The unrelenting Gardner shocked the wrestling world when he beat Karelin to take home the gold.

Top 10

1 **Vince Lombardi**
NFL, Career: 1959-69
Lombardi is the measuring stick against which all other coaches are compared. The Green Bay Packers coach won three NFL championships prior to the AFL-NFL merger, and earned victories in Super Bowls I and II. A master motivator, Lombardi is known for classic lines such as, "Winners never quit, and quitters never win."

2 **John Wooden**
College basketball, Career: 1946–75
Wooden led the UCLA Bruins to a record 10 national titles in 12 years, including seven straight from 1967 to '73. Four of his teams went undefeated and three of them had just one loss. With a 620–147 record at UCLA, Wooden holds the fourth-best winning percentage (.813) in NCAA basketball history.

3 **Phil Jackson**
NBA, Career: 1989–2011
Known as the Zen Master for his serene style, Jackson won 11 NBA titles in 20 seasons with the Chicago Bulls and Los Angeles Lakers, the most by any NBA coach. He raised the triangle offense to an art form and nurtured the games of superstars Michael Jordan, Kobe Bryant, and Shaquille O'Neal.

4 **Joe McCarthy**
MLB, Career: 1931–46
The low-key McCarthy managed the big-slugging New York Yankees of the 1930s and '40s. Those teams won eight American League pennants and seven World Series titles. McCarthy has the most wins (1,460) and the highest winning percentage (.627) of any manager in Yankees history.

5 **Mike Krzyzewski**
College basketball, Career: 1975–present
Coach K is the winningest coach in men's college basketball, with 957 victories through the 2012–13 season. Krzyzewski has made Duke into a powerhouse. In his 32 years as coach of the Blue Devils, he has won four national titles. He also led Team USA to gold medals at the 2008 and '12 Olympics.

Coaches

6 Red Auerbach
NBA, Career: 1946–66
Auerbach led the Boston Celtics to nine NBA titles. He popularized the fast break in the league and was also a pioneer in other ways. In 1950, he drafted the NBA's first African-American player, forward Chuck Cooper, and in 1964, he started five African Americans in the Celtics' lineup, an NBA first.

7 Pat Summitt
College basketball, Career: 1974–2012
Summitt is the winningest coach in NCAA basketball history, with 1,098 victories. All of Summitt's wins came at the University of Tennessee, and her eight national titles are second only to UCLA's John Wooden. Perhaps most impressive: Summitt never had a losing season in 38 years of coaching.

8 Scotty Bowman
NHL, Career: 1967–2002
With 1,244 regular-season victories, Bowman is the winningest coach in NHL history. In his first NHL coaching job he led the expansion St. Louis Blues to three straight Stanley Cup finals in their first three seasons. He later won five Cups with the Montreal Canadiens, one with the Pittsburgh Penguins, and three with the Detroit Red Wings.

9 Dan Gable
College wrestling, Career: 1976–97
Gable created a wrestling dynasty at Iowa, leading the Hawkeyes to 15 NCAA titles, including nine straight starting in 1978. Gable coached from experience. In 1972, he won a gold medal in lightweight freestyle wrestling at the Summer Olympics without surrendering a point the entire tournament.

10 Chuck Noll
NFL, Career: 1969–91
Noll took a losing Pittsburgh Steelers franchise and built it into a power. He led Pittsburgh to 11 division titles and has the most Super Bowl victories of any coach (four). He also helped advance African Americans' place in the game. Among his players were Joe Gilliam, one of the league's first starting black quarterbacks.

TOP 10
SPORTING
EVENTS

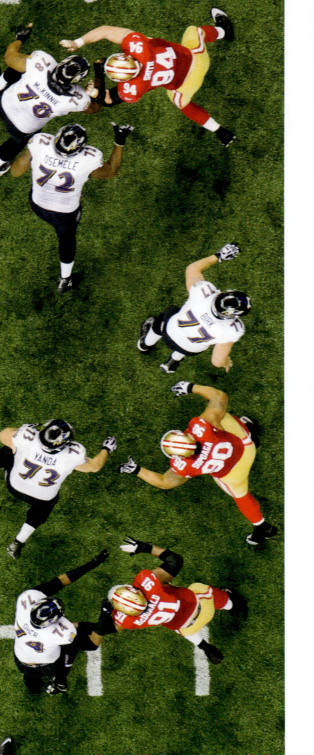

1 The Super Bowl

The Super Bowl is the biggest game in the most popular sport in the U.S. Unlike the World Series, NBA Finals, or Stanley Cup finals, one game decides the championship. The first Super Bowl didn't even sell out. But now Super Bowl Sunday has become an unofficial American holiday, with hours of pregame coverage, star-studded halftime shows, and commercial breaks that have become events unto themselves.

2 Olympic Games

Nothing brings the world together like the Olympics. After an elaborate kickoff at the opening ceremony, which features the famous lighting of the Olympic flame, the best athletes from around the globe compete for their countries. The Winter and Summer Olympics are each held once every four years. The 2012 London Games included more than 10,000 athletes from 204 different countries going for gold in 300 events.

3 World Series

The Fall Classic is the pinnacle of America's pastime. The American League and National League champions meet in a best-of-seven series that has seen some of the most famous performances in sports history, such as walk-off homers by Bill Mazeroski and Joe Carter, Babe Ruth's called shot, and a Willie Mays play known simply as "The Catch."

4 NCAA basketball tournament

The NCAA basketball tournament is also called March Madness, the most thrilling three weeks on the sports calendar. The opening Thursday and Friday have 16 games per day, all single-elimination and often between teams that have never played each other. Full of upsets and buzzer-beaters, the tournament concludes with the Final Four, featuring the teams that win each region, and the national title game.

7 FIFA World Cup

It's the biggest event of the world's most popular sport, which means much of the world stands still to tune in to the World Cup. Thirty-two teams from six regions around the world spend two years qualifying for the three-week tournament. Held only once every four years, the World Cup is the premier global sporting event after the Olympics.

8 U.S. Open

It's fitting that the final grand-slam tournament of the tennis season is played on the *hard* courts of the USTA Billie Jean King National Tennis Center, because there isn't a more difficult tournament to grind through. From the fast surface to the rowdy fans to the pressure of playing under the lights late into the night in New York City, the U.S. Open is the most electrifying tournament in all of tennis.

5 NBA Finals

The NBA's regular season consists of a grueling 82 games, but once the playoffs roll around, the players are reenergized and excitement takes over. With a combination of intense physicality and grace, the Finals is the NBA at its best. It has featured some dramatic moments, from New York Knicks center Willis Reed's Game 7 comeback after a bad injury to Chicago Bulls guard Michael Jordan's championship-clinching heroics.

6 Stanley Cup finals

The Stanley Cup is the coolest trophy in sports, so it's no surprise that NHL players battle furiously in the final series to be able to take it home. (Each member of the winning team gets to spend a day with the Cup.) The Cup was first awarded in an organized competition between leagues in 1914, when the National Hockey Association's Toronto HC swept the Pacific Coast Hockey Association's Victoria Aristocrats.

9 Kentucky Derby

Held at historic Churchill Downs, the prestigious first leg of horse racing's Triple Crown only lasts a little more than two minutes. But the Kentucky Derby is a day-long celebration filled with tradition. With fans in lavish hats, the singing of "My Old Kentucky Home," and a big garland of roses placed on the winning horse after the "Run for the Roses," the Derby is an event like no other.

10 Little League World Series

Held every year in Williamsport, Pennsylvania, the Little League World Series is one marquee event that truly puts kids in the spotlight. This is a battle of the best Little League teams from towns all around the globe. U.S. and international champions are crowned, then the two go head-to-head in a true *world* series.

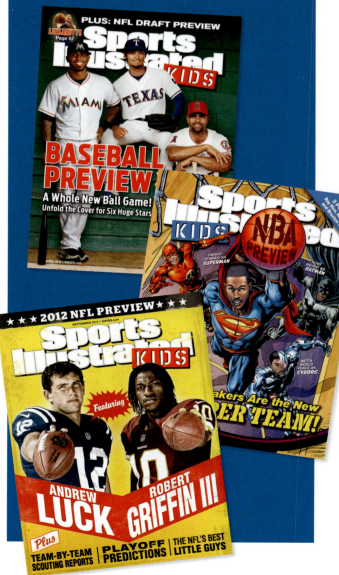